W9-ARP-759

CULTURES OF THE WORLD

CANADA

Guek-Cheng Pang

MARSHALL CAVENDISH
New York • London • Sydney

Reference edition published 1994 by
Marshall Cavendish Corporation
2415 Jerusalem Avenue
P.O. Box 587
North Bellmore
New York 11710

© Times Editions Pte Ltd 1994

Originated and designed by
Times Books International, an imprint of
Times Editions Pte Ltd

Printed in Singapore

Library of Congress Cataloging-in-Publication Data:
Cheng, Pang Guek.
    Canada / Pang Guek Cheng
      p. cm.—(Cultures Of The World)
    Includes bibliographical references (p.) and index.
    Summary: Examines the geography, history,
    government, economy, and culture of Canada.
    ISBN 1-85435-579-1
    1. Canada—Juvenile literature [1. Canada.]
I. Title. II. Series.
F1008.2.C44 1993
971—dc20   93–10018
                    CIP
                     AC

Cultures of the World

Editorial Director	Shirley Hew
Managing Editor	Shova Loh
Editors	Michael Spilling
	Winnifred Wong
	Falak Kagda
	Roslind Varghese
	Jenny Goh
	Sue Sismondo
Picture Editor	Yee May Kaung
Production	Edmund Lam
Design	Tuck Loong
	Ronn Yeo
	Felicia Wong
	Loo Chuan Ming
Illustrators	Jimmy Kang
	Andrew Leong
	Anuar bin Abdul Rahim
MCC Editorial Director	Evelyn M. Fazio

INTRODUCTION

TO THE REST of the world, Canada is seen chiefly as some kind of younger cousin to the United States. Americans perhaps think of Canada as their backyard and Canadians as poorer relatives for whom they hold much affection. Canadians themselves are sure they have their own, separate identity, distinct from their neighbor to the south. It may not be easy to describe to others what it is that makes one Canadian, but Canadians do know they are *not* American in their way of thinking. This distinctiveness cannot be perceived with a cursory glance, but only becomes obvious upon closer examination. Whether of native, European, or Asian origin, Canada's people are a diverse lot who have come together, not in a melting pot that blends their separate flavors into one whole, but in a mosaic rich with many different distinct colors and textures.

CONTENTS

Farmers have their lunch in Saskatchewan, one of the main grain-growing regions of Canada.

CONTENTS

Deer hunters seek out their quarry near White-court in Alberta.

GEOGRAPHY

CANADA IS THE SECOND-LARGEST country in the world. It covers nearly 3.8 million square miles and is larger than both the United States (by 200,000 square miles) and China. Only Russia is bigger than Canada. In spite of its size, Canada is one of the least populated countries in the world.

Politically, Canada is divided into 10 provinces and two territories. Each province administers its own natural resources. The territories are controlled by the federal government because of their remoteness and small population.

SIX REGIONS

Geographically, Canada can be grouped into six regional areas:

The Appalachian Region (Newfoundland, Prince Edward Island, Nova Scotia, New Brunswick, and the southeast extremity of Quebec) is characterized by forested hills and a rugged and indented coastline washed by the Atlantic Ocean. The Great Lakes-St. Lawrence lowlands is a small area of Canada, part of the provinces of Ontario and Quebec, yet it is a rich, highly agricultural and commercial area and home to more than half of Canada's population. To the north of the lowlands, occupying about half the mainland of Canada, is the Canadian Shield, an ancient, glacially eroded region full of rivers, lakes, and forests. Its practically uninhabitable nature is responsible for pressing the population close to the United States' border. The interior plains or prairies are the largest area of nearly flat land in Canada. It is bounded on the west by the Rocky Mountains and on the east by the Canadian Shield. To the west is the Western Cordillera, a region of mountains, plateaus, and valleys that extend from the Rocky Mountains to the Coast Mountains rising from the Pacific Ocean, and north through the Yukon Territory into Alaska. The sixth region is the North, a resource-rich but harsh and essentially treeless environment with an arctic climate.

Opposite: **The Mackenzie River delta in the Northwest Territories.**

PROVINCE BY PROVINCE

NEWFOUNDLAND The most easterly of the provinces is Newfoundland ("NOOF-n-land"). The larger, mainland part of the province is called Labrador, a mostly barren land of rocks, swamps, and lakes. Its rugged coastline has promontories that rise directly from the sea. The people here live extremely isolated lives and often have to travel from place to place by water.

The island of Newfoundland is also very mountainous and has a rocky, rugged coastline. There are few big cities, and life is centered around small fishing villages. The coastal waters are rich in fish, especially cod.

The land is also rich in minerals, and the processing of its abundant natural resources is an important part of the province's economy. Iron ore provides Labrador's greatest source of wealth. Pulp and paper and food processing are the main manufacturing industries.

The capital of Newfoundland is St. John's. It is the oldest city in North America and was England's first overseas colony, the very beginnings of the British Empire.

PRINCE EDWARD ISLAND Prince Edward Island, or PEI as it is known, is the country's smallest but most densely populated province. Its rich, red soil supports a mainly farming community that produces potatoes as its main crop. Fishing, especially for lobsters, is another important industry.

St. John's, Newfoundland, was one of the first places in Canada to be colonized by British settlers.

The capital of PEI is Charlottetown. It is known as the "Cradle of Confederation," because it was the site of the historic meeting in 1864 that eventually led to the unification of Canada in 1867.

NOVA SCOTIA Nova Scotia lies on a peninsula, surrounded by the waters of the Bay of Fundy, the Atlantic Ocean, the Gulf of St. Lawrence, and the Northumberland Strait. Like its neighboring provinces, it has a rugged coastline cut by numerous bays and inlets—ideal sites for fishing villages. The Nova Scotia fishery is one of Canada's largest. Agriculture, the raising of livestock, and fruit growing are also important.

Productive forests occupy about 75% of Nova Scotia. Only about one quarter of this woodland is state owned, much of which is used for public parks and reserves. Because of this, hunting—especially for deer and moose—is a favorite outdoor sport for tourists and Nova Scotians alike.

The province was mainly settled by people who came from England and Scotland. Nova Scotia means "New Scotland" in Latin, and the Scottish influence is strong here.

Halifax, the capital, has one of the best natural harbors in the world and is the headquarters of Canada's small navy. It is a major port.

If the 26 million people who live in Canada were to be evenly spread out, there would be roughly seven people per square mile. In fact, as much as 89% of the country is unpopulated and two-thirds of the population live within 125 miles of the border with the United States.

NEW BRUNSWICK Nearly rectangular in shape and with an extensive coastline, New Brunswick is an undulating, heavily forested land. Forest products and food processing are the main manufacturing industries.

An interesting physical phenomenon occurs in this province—the bore tide on the Bay of Fundy that New Brunswick shares with Nova Scotia. When the incoming tide reaches its peak, it creates a wall of water which roars all at once up the bay towards the towns of Moncton, New Brunswick, and Truro, Nova Scotia. This happens twice a day, and visitors can stand on special viewing platforms to watch the bore advance.

Fredericton is the capital of New Brunswick, and Saint John is its main port and industrial center.

Horseshoe Falls in Ontario. This is part of the world-famous Niagara Falls, a breathtaking attraction Canada shares with the United States.

QUEBEC This is the largest of the provinces. Physically, it is made up of three regions—the plateau-like highlands of the Canadian Shield in the north, the Appalachian Mountains that extend through the area south of the St. Lawrence River, and the St. Lawrence lowlands.

The lowlands are a fertile area where agriculture was once the mainstay of life. Agriculture is still important today, though it has been overtaken by manufacturing, especially the textile and clothing industries. Quebec is also a major producer of gold, iron ore, copper, and asbestos.

The mainly French population has a culture that sets it apart from the rest of Canada. The capital of Quebec is Quebec City, a city with a rather European and Old World atmosphere. Montreal, Quebec's largest city, is a great industrial, commercial, and financial center.

ONTARIO Ontario is made up of the Canadian Shield in the north and the Great Lakes-St. Lawrence lowlands in the south. While the north is a rugged, rocky, and inhospitable land, the lowlands support a dense and highly industrialized population, which accounts for about half of Canadian manufacturing.

Toronto, Canada's most cosmopolitan city. The CN Tower, at 1,815 feet, dominates the skyline.

The cluster of cities around the western end of Lake Ontario is known as Canada's "golden horseshoe." It includes Hamilton (center of Canada's iron and steel manufacture), Oshawa (center of the automobile industry), and Toronto.

Ontario is Canada's richest province, and about a third of all Canadians live here. Ethnically, it is also the most diverse. All kinds of people live here, French and English mixing with many other Europeans and Asians.

Cosmopolitan Toronto, Ontario's capital, is Canada's largest city, and its financial and business center. Ottawa, near Ontario's southeastern border with Quebec, is the capital of Canada.

MANITOBA Northeastern Manitoba is part of the Canadian Shield and is hilly and forested; the southwestern part is flat.

The economy of Manitoba has been built on agriculture, mainly the growing of wheat and other grain crops. Winnipeg, the capital, is the industrial center of the province. It was the first stop in the great rush for land by European settlers who followed the railroad west. Today, it is still home to their descendants—Ukrainians, Hungarians, Poles, Jews, Italians, and Portuguese.

SASKATCHEWAN This is the great grain-producing region of Canada. Two-thirds of the province is flat, prairie lowland, where most of Canada's wheat crop is grown.

The province is also rich in mineral resources, especially potash (Saskatchewan is a major world producer of potash), oil, and metals (notably uranium). The cities of Regina, the capital, and Saskatoon are distribution centers for the surrounding rural areas.

ALBERTA Alberta lies mainly in Canada's interior plains region. The southern part of the province is a dry and treeless prairie. From Alberta's border with Saskatchewan in the east, the land rises gradually until it meets the Rocky Mountains in the west.

From this province comes half of the value of all the minerals produced in Canada, mainly petroleum, natural gas and its by-products, and coal. Agriculture is also important, especially grain and livestock. Edmonton is Alberta's capital and its largest city. Calgary is the second-largest city in Alberta.

BRITISH COLUMBIA Also known as BC, British Columbia is almost completely made up of the Cordilleran region of parallel mountain ranges that run north-south.

The Rocky Mountains, which continue southward into Washington State in the United States, are a continuous range of wall-like ridges, carved by glaciation. The central section consists of several mountain ranges, plateaus and lake basins. In the west are the Coast Mountains. The Inside Passage and the Strait of Georgia, which separate the Queen Charlotte Islands and Vancouver Island from the mainland, together form one of the finest natural waterways in the world.

Vancouver is the province's largest city, a rapidly growing cosmopolitan home to immigrants from all over the world. Victoria, the provincial capital, is BC's second-largest city. It is on the southern tip of Vancouver Island.

YUKON AND NORTHWEST TERRITORIES "Yukon" is an Indian name that means "greatest," and so it is—full of jagged mountains, boundless waterways, and sharply contrasting seasons. The Northwest Territories, or NWT, is equally magnificent and covers an area roughly one-third the size of the whole country.

Mount Logan, the highest mountain in Canada (19,524 feet), is in the Yukon, and the Mackenzie River, the longest river in Canada (1,060 miles), is in the NWT. The whole region is north of latitude 60°, and part of it is within the Arctic Circle. The Alaska Highway, which is 1,388 miles long, begins at Dawson Creek in BC and ends at Fairbanks, Alaska. This is the best road access to the Yukon. Whitehorse is the capital of the Yukon, and Yellowknife is the capital of the NWT.

Located at Watson's Lake, Yukon Territory, this "signpost forest" contains contributions from all over the world.

Quebec City, the oldest city in Canada, is situated on the St. Lawrence River.

ST. LAWRENCE SEAWAY The St. Lawrence Seaway is a system of locks, canals, and channels that link the Great Lakes with the Atlantic Ocean. The cost of constructing the seaway was divided between Canada and the United States. The waterway is 2,355 miles long from the Atlantic Ocean to the northern tip of Lake Superior. It now permits ocean-going ships to sail from Montreal across Lake Superior to Duluth, Minnesota.

Construction of the seaway was a monumental feat of engineering. The Montreal-Lake Ontario section, which is often thought of as the whole seaway, has four locks that together lift a ship traveling westward about 213 feet. Between Lake Ontario and Lake Erie, the Welland Canal circumvents Niagara Falls.

A NEW TERRITORY

For the first time since 1949, when Newfoundland became Canada's 10th province, the map of Canada could change. In 1992, the Inuit people in the eastern part of the Northwest Territories voted 69% in favor of setting up a new territory called Nunavut (a word which means "our land" in Inuktitut, the Inuit language). Once Parliament gives final approval to this land claim settlement, the Inuit will be granted title to (and the right to hunt, fish, and trap in) 135,000 square miles of land. They will also receive $1.2 billion over 14 years. The territory will be run by Canada's first aboriginal self-government.

The seaway is vital to the Canadian economy, opening the interior of the continent to ocean-going ships and allowing direct, energy-efficient transport of materials such as iron ore, grain, and coal.

COLD, HOT, WET, AND DRY

The climate in Canada varies considerably from region to region, from an arctic extreme where temperatures are often below freezing most of the year, to the southern regions where the milder seasons of spring, summer, and fall remain for at least eight months of the year.

Atlantic Canada has a fairly changeable climate. There is often a lot of snow in winter, and fog is common in spring and summer. Central Canada, from the Great Lakes to the Rocky Mountains, experiences a continental climate with cold winters and hot summers and light, unreliable rainfall. Southern Ontario and Quebec, where the Great Lakes-St. Lawrence lowlands are located, have cold winters with heavy snowfall and hot but fairly wet summers.

The northernmost extremes of the Northwest Territories offer awe-inspiring vistas of glaciers, cliffs, and fjords, all monuments of the Ice Age.

On the west coast, the climate is the most temperate because airstreams from the Pacific Ocean keep winters mild, though cloudy and wet.

In the north, areas within the Arctic Circle experience extremely long, cold winters and only a few months with above-freezing temperatures.

Over the years Canadians have learned to live with and develop a healthy respect for their climate. When they are indoors, the marvels of central heating in winter and air conditioning in summer insulate them from the extremes of the weather. When outdoors, dressing properly for protection against the cold is important.

The evergreen forest of Banff national park in Alberta. The park was created in 1885 as Canada's first national park.

FORESTS AND GRASSLANDS

Canada is a country rich in natural resources, not the least of which are its abundant forests. Today, in spite of much clearing of the land for urbanization, there are still forests everywhere (nearly a third of Canada is forested)—from the undeveloped frontiers of the north to the outskirts of the largest cities.

Most of Canada's forests lie within the northern regions, stretching from Newfoundland to Alaska and continuing in western Canada on the slopes of the Rockies and parallel mountain ranges. They are composed mainly of evergreens or conifers (cone-bearing trees) like firs, spruce, and pine.

Temperate forests of broad-leaved deciduous trees, which shed their leaves in the fall, such as oak, maple, elm, beech, and ash, are found in the southern, milder parts of the country. On the west coast, the mild and wet climate supports the growth of dense forests of tall trees—the Douglas fir, Sitka spruce, and western red cedar. The Douglas fir is Canada's tallest species of tree, growing to more than 200 feet.

In the interior, where rainfall is light and evaporation greatest, grasses grow ranging from six inches to as tall as eight feet. These grasslands cover most of the prairie provinces and the drier sections of interior British Columbia. They are suited to the dry climate—their abundant roots readily absorb moisture, narrow leaves conserve moisture, and slender, flexible stalks bend with the wind.

In the very cold parts of the country, in the arctic and alpine regions, are tundra meadows of coarse grasses, mosses, and lichens. Few trees grow here because of the severe climate.

FROM PYGMY SHREW TO GREAT BLUE WHALE

Animal life in Canada is extremely diverse and varies dramatically from region to region. On the one hand is the pygmy shrew, the smallest mammal in Canada; on the other, the great blue whale, which can grow up to 100 feet long and weigh 150 tons, and is the largest creature known to man.

Most animals in Canada adapt to the cold winters in a variety of ways. Some migrate south in the fall, some grow a thick winter coat of fur or feathers, and others hibernate, living off a thick layer of fat.

The inland waters and the seas around Canada support teeming colonies of microscopic plankton and the great number of fishes, amphibians, and marine mammals that depend on them. The grasslands support grass eaters, such as deer. The forests provide food for rabbits, squirrels, and rodents. Some birds of prey, like hawks and eagles, remain in Canada all year round, while others, like the insect eaters, fly south in the winter.

A bison ranch in Alberta. Although bison are as large as domestic cattle, and eat only as a third as much, they have an unpredictable temperament that makes them difficult to domesticate.

People, in their colonization of the land, have been responsible for the extinction of many species. Some, like the Great Plains wolf, the Dawson caribou, the sea mink, and the great auk (a penguin-like bird), were hunted out of existence. Others, like the greater prairie chicken, declined in numbers because of the destruction of their natural habitat.

But today, amidst growing environmental concern, strict hunting regulations and conservation efforts are turning the tide. Musk oxen, whooping crane, and the bald eagle are protected species. There were once fewer than a thousand musk oxen and American bison, but the protection of the law has brought them back from the verge of extinction.

BEARS

There are three types of bears found in Canada. The most familiar is the black bear, which can be found almost everywhere in the country except in the extreme north.

Black bears, which are sometimes brown in color, are good climbers. They are omnivorous and will eat almost anything they can find. Vegetation forms a large part of their diet, especially berries and nuts in the summer. Bears are also fond of scavenging in garbage and will gather where there is refuse. This brings them in close contact with people. Black bears are normally shy animals, but those that have developed the habit of feeding on garbage sometimes become a nuisance and a danger to people.

The grizzly bear is found in western Alberta, British Columbia, the Yukon, and the Northwest Territories. It is much larger than the black bear and has a characteristic hump over the shoulders formed by the muscles of its forelegs. It gets its name from the light or grizzled fur on the head and shoulders. The grizzly is also omnivorous, often digging for roots, but it will also prey on elk, moose, deer, and caribou.

Polar bears inhabit the arctic sea coast. They vary in color from almost pure white in winter to a yellow or golden color in summer and fall. Their thick winter coats and a thick layer of fat under the skin protect them from the cold. They are more carnivorous than the grizzly or black bear, preying mostly on seals.

TIME ZONES

Before 1884, local time in Canada was determined by setting noon as the moment when the sun was directly overhead. But because this moment is reached at different times in the various parts of the country, local time varied considerably across Canada. This was not a problem until the railway made it possible for people to travel quickly over long distances. This method of calculating local time made it difficult to work out train schedules.

The problem was solved in 1884 when the system of Standard Time was adopted. This divided Canada into different time zones.

Today, Canada has six time zones—from east to west, these are: Newfoundland, Atlantic, Eastern, Central, Mountain and Pacific Standard Times. The difference between one time zone and the next is one hour, except for the difference between Atlantic Standard Time and Newfoundland Standard Time, which is half an hour.

In 1918, Daylight Saving Time was introduced to give Canadians an extra hour of daylight each day during the summer. Daylight Saving Time comes into effect on the first Sunday in April when clocks are put forward an hour. On the last Sunday in October, all the nation's clocks are reset to Standard Time.

Canada's six time zones: the hours indicated in each shows how many hours the zone is behind Greenwich Mean Time.

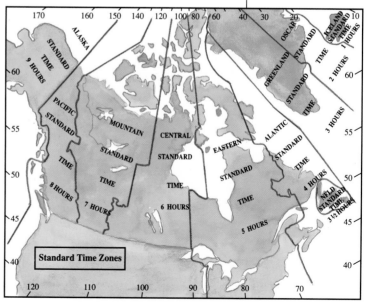

Standard Time Zones

HISTORY

CANADA'S HISTORY is one of immigration and settlement. The 10 provinces and two territories that stretch from the Atlantic to the Pacific Ocean are home to peoples that came from many lands.

While there have been no great wars of independence or civil strife, these people have over time struggled with nature and overcome differences among themselves to create a nation with a common identity and vision. Nevertheless, tensions remain that even today need to be resolved.

THE FIRST PEOPLE

Most anthropologists agree that Canada's first people crossed the Bering Strait from Asia more than 25,000 years ago during the Ice Age. They came over a land bridge that then joined Asia and North America. These first immigrants were nomads who traveled the land hunting animals for food. As the weather warmed up and the ice melted, animals and people moved south into the heart of North America. Eventually, the people learned to gather wild plants and cultivate the rich earth; they stopped their wanderings and became the first settlers of the land.

The first people developed many cultures, societies, and linguistic groups. They were called Indians by the European explorers who came looking for a western route to India. Their own names for themselves, such as Dene, Nahani, and Kutchin, simply meant "the people."

Their culture varied as widely as the terrain of Canada itself. In the interior plains, groups of families lived in a migratory manner, hunting buffalo for meat and skins. The plains Indians were the Blackfoot, Blood, Piegan, Gros Ventre, Cree, Sioux, and Assiniboin. They lived in tepees— conical shelters covered with skins—which were portable and easily erected, yet warm and sound enough to withstand strong winds.

Opposite: **A statue in Quebec City of the city's founding father, the explorer Samuel de Champlain.**

Those on the west coast—the Haida, Tsimshian, Nootka, Coast Salish, Kwakiutl, and Bella Coola—established permanent villages and lived off the bounty of the sea, fishing for salmon and hunting whales. Their houses, built from cedar, were huge. They had the leisure time to carve huge totem poles and other art objects from cedar and stone.

Also unique were the nomadic woodland peoples of the east—the Algonkians, Micmac, Montagnais, Naskapi, Ojibway and Cree—who lived in lodges and wigwams, homes constructed of poles, bark, and skins. They were hunters and trappers who followed the animals wherever they went.

The Iroquoian hunters of southern Ontario—the Huron, Tobacco Nation, Neutrals, Mohawk, Oneida, Onondaga, Cayuga, Seneca and Tuscarora—were superb farmers. They grew corn, beans, and squash and lived in permanent villages of longhouses.

The tribes of the interior plateau were the Interior Salish, Kootenay, Chilcotin, Carrier, and Tagish Indians. They hunted and fished for food. Their dwellings ranged from subterranean pits to buffalo-hide tepees.

Finally, the native people of the far north were the Inuit (the name they gave themselves, meaning "the people"), who hunted caribou, whales, and seals. They lived in snow houses called igloos that protected them from the cold. Once inside, a small oil lamp and body heat kept them comfortably warm.

Warm in winter and cool in summer, the tepee is able to withstand gale-force winds and yet is easily dismantled for travel purposes.

All these cultures had in common a deep, spiritual relationship with the land and with nature. When the Europeans arrived, they brought conflict and diseases that caused devastation among the native people. For decades, the native population declined, and the existence of their unique cultures was threatened.

ARRIVAL OF THE EUROPEANS

It is not known when the first Europeans came to North America, but there are ancient legends that tell of travelers from Scandinavia who found a new western continent long before Christopher Columbus did. There is archeological evidence that a Viking adventurer called Leif Ericson established a colony on the shores of Newfoundland for a short time. For centuries after the Vikings, there was very little European exploration of the new continent, until the search for a new sea route to the East led to the discovery of America by Christopher Columbus.

When news of the vastness and riches of the new land reached Europe, it attracted many other European adventurers. But there was little impact on the natives of Canada (even the word Canada is derived from the Indian word "kanata") until the first colonizers—French adventurers and explorers—arrived.

The most northerly of the Inuit (Eskimo) people traditionally lived in igloos constructed from blocks of ice.

"Now, God be praised, I will die in peace," said the dying James Wolfe to his officers on the Plain of Abraham.

FRENCH-ENGLISH RIVALRY

In the early stages of the struggle for control of the continent, the French outdid the English. French explorers such as Jacques Cartier and Samuel de Champlain, soldiers, missionaries, and the *coureurs de bois* ("koo-RER de bwah," literally runners and hunters of the woods)—adventurous fur traders— opened up North America. They were lured by the belief that the new land they had discovered was rich in gold. They were also driven by the idea of bringing salvation and civilization to the "savages" they found there, as well as gaining new land and glory for their king. Although they did not find gold, the French found that the new land was rich in something almost as valuable—an almost inexhaustible supply of fur, especially of beaver pelts.

By the 1670s, the empire that they established, called New France, stretched from as far north as the Hudson Bay in the Arctic to the Gulf of Mexico in the south. It was run on a seigneurial system, which means the French settlers were granted land by the French Crown in return for military service. No more than 10,000 immigrants came to settle during the entire history of New France, yet they prospered in this new land, growing to a population of 60,000 by 1760.

EMPIRE BUILDER

In 1534, French explorer and navigator Jacques Cartier sailed into the Gulf of St. Lawrence and landed on the Gaspé Peninsula. Planting a great cross, he claimed the land for France and for God. In 1535, Cartier made his second voyage up the St. Lawrence River to the site of the present-day Montreal. He became the first European to enter the Canadian interior. On his third voyage to the new land, in 1541, Cartier established a settlement, but this colony lasted only until 1543. Cartier and many other French explorers helped build a vast empire in North America called New France.

THE *COUREURS DE BOIS*

"We were Caesars, being nobody to contradict us," said French explorer and trader Pierre-Esprit Radisson, in 1661, describing the life of the *coureurs de bois*. The *coureurs de bois* were the backbone of the early trading system. They were bold, boisterous adventurers who trapped animals while living a precarious existence in the wild. Many had come from France to escape a life of drudgery. Some had exchanged prison sentences for emigration papers.

Pressure on New France came from English settlements to the south and east, because French-controlled lands blocked the expansion westward of the English colonies on the eastern seaboard. In the north, the French faced rivalry from the Hudson's Bay Company for dominance of the fur trade. As a result, New France and the English fought an almost continuous series of battles in the 17th and 18th centuries in which the various Indian tribes allied themselves with one or the other.

The end of New France finally came in 1759 with the fall of the city of Quebec in which British sea power played a big part. The British navy, controlling the Atlantic, cut the colony of New France off from the mother country. With troops on board commanded by England's youngest general, 32-year-old James Wolfe, a British fleet sailed down the St. Lawrence River for Quebec. The battle raged for many months, climaxing on the Plains of Abraham, west of the city. Wolfe's men formed their famous "thin red line" across the plains while the French forces, under the command of the Marquis de Montcalm, advanced. When the battle was over, the Plains of Abraham were covered with the fallen French. Both commanders were mortally wounded. Wolfe lived just long enough to learn he had won the battle, while Montcalm died a few hours later. In 1763, France ceded its North American territories to Britain through the Treaty of Paris.

The death of General Montcalm after the French defeat at the Battle of Quebec in 1759.

An old cannon from the French-Indian Wars, facing out into the St. Lawrence River from the *Chateau Coteau du Lac* in Quebec.

INVASION AND IMMIGRATION

The new imperial rulers found themselves masters of a population that was different in language and religion. To prevent an uprising, Governor Sir Guy Carleton concluded that French civil and religious rights had to be upheld. In the Quebec Act of 1774, therefore, legal status was given to the Roman Catholic Church, to the seigneurial system of landholding, and to French civil law.

When the 13 colonies in North America revolted against British rule in the mid-1770s, Quebec was expected to join the uprising. But this did not happen because the French, who were staunch Royalists and devout Catholics, had little love for the Protestant republicans in the south. America gained independence, but Britain still reigned supreme in the north. The American Revolution had a dramatic side effect. Thousands of Americans who had been faithful to England migrated north. Most of these United Empire Loyalists populated the mainly empty shores of Nova Scotia, creating a new colony called New Brunswick, while others settled along the north shore of Lake Ontario.

These new British settlers soon changed the way that Canada was governed. Being used to representative institutions, the Loyalists chafed under French seigneurial and civil law. To avoid conflict, in 1791, Britain created two colonies, Upper and Lower Canada. Upper Canada was controlled by these Loyalist elements while Lower Canada, with the city of Quebec as its center, remained essentially French in character.

Meanwhile, antagonism between Britain and the United States continued. Much of the conflict was caused by British insistence on retaining control over shipping in the St. Lawrence River and the Great Lakes.

Invasion and Immigration

The years of friction culminated in the War of 1812, when an American army marched up the banks of the Richelieu River, only to be pushed back by the British. It was the only time that Canada and the United States fought with each other. After several skirmishes, in which neither side won, the war ended with the Treaty of Ghent in 1814. Britain and the United States agreed to demilitarize the Great Lakes and extend the border along the 49th parallel to the Rockies.

After the war, the British government, in an effort to strengthen the colonies, helped immigrants to settle in British North America. Others came of their own accord, fleeing the poverty of the early stages of the Industrial Revolution, the starvation wages in bleak factory towns, and an impoverished life on farms. Between 1815 and 1855, a million Britons arrived at Halifax, St. John, and Quebec. These immigrants changed the ethnic composition of the country, turning the French-speaking population into the minority.

In Lower Canada, the French showed their discontent with several uprisings against British domination. The rebellion of 1837 brought Lord Durham from Britain to investigate the cause of the political unrest. He recommended that the two provinces be joined once again into a united Province of Canada. Durham thought unity was the best way to bring Canada's economic progress up to the level of the more dynamic United States. The Province of Canada was created in 1841.

Halifax in Nova Scotia was a popular place for immigrants to settle in the 19th century.

THE HUDSON'S BAY COMPANY

The green, red, yellow, and blue stripes of The Bay are prominent in the shopping centers of many towns and cities in Canada. The company is the modern-day child of the Hudson's Bay Company, the oldest incorporated merchandising company in the English-speaking world. The Hudson's Bay Company played a very important part in the opening up of Canada, especially in the north and west of the country. It was originally a fur trading company, exploiting the interior of the continent from Hudson's Bay in the north.

In 1670, King Charles II of England signed a royal charter granting the "Governor and Company of Adventurers" wide powers, including exclusive trading rights in the vast territory that was drained by rivers flowing into Hudson Bay. This region was called Rupert's Land. The company fought with the French for control of the fur trade until 1713 when France acknowledged England's claim to Hudson Bay in the Treaty of Utrecht. In 1821, the Hudson's Bay Company extended its monopoly to the west when it merged with its former rival, the North West Company. For almost two centuries, the company not only controlled the fur trade but effectively ruled the land, being responsible for providing law and order and government in the region. When it sold Rupert's Land to Canada in 1870, the company retained much of the land on which it had its trading posts and large areas of the prairies. It became increasingly involved in real estate, at the same time doing much business with settlers through the trading posts it had retained.

Competition for the Hudson's Bay Company was provided by the rival North West Company (founded in 1783), who established themselves in Manitoba. Conflict between the two trading rivals occasionally broke out, leading to killings on both sides. In 1821, the two were merged under the Hudson's Bay Company by the British government to diffuse the hostilities.

MÉTIS OF MANITOBA

The Métis were a people created by the union of French trappers and native Indian women. They were hunters and trackers, with a French and Catholic heritage, who lived a semi-nomadic way of life hunting buffalo. But the buffalo dwindled as the railroad opened up the west. Afraid their rights might be ignored, the Métis, under their charismatic leader Louis Riel, revolted and forced the federal government to grant provincial status to Manitoba. Peace was restored for a while, but in 1885 the Métis rebelled again. This time they were crushed and Riel was executed.

THE BIRTH OF A NATION

At this time, the colonies of New Brunswick, Nova Scotia, Prince Edward Island, and Newfoundland had little to do with the Province of Canada and were attracting their share of settlers from both the French and British communities. They were under the direct control of the British government in London. The 1840s and 1850s were a period of rapid change for all. Britain adopted a free-trade policy and granted the provinces self-government in local matters. This caused the colonies to develop closer economic ties with the United States.

In 1864, when the leaders of the three maritime provinces of Nova Scotia, New Brunswick, and Prince Edward Island decided to discuss the possibility of a union of their three provinces, United Canada saw this as an opportunity to present a grander proposal—that of the union of all five into a much larger country, Canada. The political situation after the American Civil War in the 1860s had much to do with the birth of the new nation. There was an increased threat that the American army might turn its attention to the British colonies in the north. This, coupled with the British desire to see its colonies take greater responsibility for their own affairs, added the finishing touches to the plan.

In 1866, the provinces of Nova Scotia, New Brunswick, and United Canada sent delegates to England to present their proposals to the British Parliament. There, agreement was reached and Parliament passed the British North America Act, which came into effect on July 1, 1867, creating the Dominion of Canada. These provinces were later joined by the provinces of Manitoba, British Columbia, Prince Edward Island, Alberta, Saskatchewan, and Newfoundland.

A WORLD POWER

"Geography has made us neighbors. History has made us friends. Economics has made us partners. And necessity has made us allies."

—Speech by John F. Kennedy to a joint session of the Senate and House of Commons in Ottawa in 1961.

Despite Confederation, internal Canadian politics were occupied for many years with the problem of francophone (French-speaking people) rights outside of Quebec. Canada continued to attract large numbers of immigrants who filled the cities and farmed the land. Canadian resources such as wheat, forest products, and minerals supplied a world market, and the country became prosperous in the early decades of the 20th century.

The sensitive issue of francophone rights flared again and divided Canadians deeply during World War I when the federal government decided it had to boost military ranks with enforced conscription. French Canadians were violently opposed to this, seeing it as a move to reduce their already declining numbers. Canadian unity was strained almost to the breaking point. The war took a great toll, as more than 60,000 Canadians died in battle. But with the end of hostilities, prosperity returned. There

Men of the Canadian 48th Highlanders in action in Europe in 1944.

War memorial in Ottawa commemorating those who died in the two World Wars.

was an acceleration of industrial development. New resources like lead and zinc and new products like the automobile and radio found expanding markets at home and abroad.

The Great Depression of the 1930s hit Canada, which suffered one financial crisis after another, until the outbreak of World War II changed the situation. Once again, Canadian troops saw action overseas, playing a major role in defeating enemy forces in Italy and in the Allied landings at Normandy, France. Canada provided munitions and food supplies to the Allied war effort. By the end of the war, more than 42,000 Canadians had died. The wartime effort, however, helped Canada to join the ranks of the world's industrialized powers, since the economy had grown and new industries had developed. Post-war immigration doubled the population and provided the labor needed to work the newly-developed industries.

Both politically and economically, Canada developed close relations with the United States that have remained to this day. During the Cold War years, the threat of living next to the Soviet communist superpower forced Canada to be almost totally dependent on the United States for her defense.

HISTORY OF INDIAN POLICY

Unlike in the United States, where the wild West and its cowboys and Indians were very much a part of American history, there were little or no hostilities between the Indians and the white settlers in Canada. From the very beginning, both the British and French were interested in getting Indian cooperation to help them with their fur trading. Then, as they became interested in working the land, they sought to take the land from the Indians, not through wars and fighting, but through a series of treaty agreements. Through these agreements, the Indians surrendered their rights to the land in return for special reserve lands that were set aside entirely for their use. Between 1764 and 1862, 31 treaties were signed, mostly covering the fertile agricultural lands on the north shore of Lake Ontario. After Confederation, between 1871 and 1921, another 11 treaties opened up land for new settlers from coast to coast.

The Indian Act of 1876 gave the government great powers to control Indians living on reservations, generally by governing all aspects of Indian life in the hope that eventually they would become assimilated into the rest of society. Even when it was revised in 1951, the Indian Act was still very restrictive. It distinguished between status and non-status Indians (those who were registered with the government as Indians and those who were not) and discriminated against Indian women by taking away their Indian status if they married a non-Indian. Through a government residential school system, Indian children were forcibly taken away from their families, continuing the

A Canadian Indian protests for his rights on the back of his T-shirt!

32

QUEBEC SEPARATISM

Separatism is a term meaning the advocacy of separation or secession by a group from a larger political unit to which it belongs.

In Canada, this term is commonly associated with the aspirations of those French-speaking people of Quebec who see separatism as the means of stopping the decline of their culture and language in a continent that is largely English-dominated. This philosophy is embodied by the political party, Parti Québécois, which was formed in 1968. The party is committed to a program of "sovereignty-association," that is, it espouses political independence from Canada while retaining some links, such as a common currency. Popular support for the Parti Québécois resulted in the party being swept to power in 1976, and again in 1981. Yet, in 1980, when asked in a province-wide referendum whether they would support sovereignty-association negotiations with the rest of Canada, the people of Quebec said no.

During the recent constitutional crisis of 1992, Canadians as a whole and the people of Quebec themselves rejected a new constitutional accord that had been put together by their political leaders. This raised the specter of separatism once again; some political analysts have interpreted this rejection as being the first step to the inevitable separation of Quebec from Canada. Only time will tell if Canada will remain intact.

process of assimilation. In the late 1940s, Indian leaders spoke out against this policy and expressed their people's desire to regain their rightful position of equality with Canadians of other races. Accordingly, in 1970, the government began helping Indian groups and associations research the treaties and Indian rights.

In 1972, the National Indian Brotherhood (now the Assembly of First Nations) asked that Indians be given control over their own education, so that Indian children could be taught their culture and traditions. This proposal was adopted in 1973 by the Department of Indian Affairs and Northern Development. At the same time, the Canadian government announced its willingness to consider Indian claims. This willingness to discuss native rights and titles to land, resources, and self-government is an attitude that continues to this day.

GOVERNMENT

Canada is, geographically, the largest democratic country in the world. It is a constant challenge to make that democracy work in a country that is so large and populated with people of such diverse backgrounds.

When, on July 1, 1867, Canada became a nation, it also became a democratic federation. This means that the powers of government are shared between a central or federal government and the governments of the various provinces that make up the nation. The Constitution Act of 1867, also called the British North America Act, 1867, established one Parliament for Canada consisting of the British monarch, the Senate, and the House of Commons.

THE BRITISH CROWN AND ITS REPRESENTATIVES

The queen of Canada, who is also the queen of England, is the head of state. This makes Canada a constitutional monarchy, unlike the United States, which is a republic. In Canada, the prime minister is the head of government while the queen is the head of state. In the United States, the president is both the head of government as well as the head of state. As the head of state, the queen can protect Parliament and the people against any abuse of powers by the prime minister and his cabinet. As the queen does not live in Canada, she appoints a governor general to represent her on the advice of the prime minister.

The governor general is appointed for five years. He or she does not have any real power—this lies with the government—and is not involved in party politics. The governor general gives "royal assent" to acts of Parliament, signs state documents, appoints the leader of the political party in power as prime minister, opens, discontinues, or dissolves Parliament on the advice of the prime minister, and reads the "speech from the throne" at the opening of a new Parliament and at every new session of Parliament.

Opposite: **Parliament buildings in Ottawa. These were rebuilt after a fire in 1916, in a Gothic revival style.**

One of the most important duties of a governor general is to ensure that the country is never without a leader. When a prime minister dies or resigns suddenly, the governor general appoints someone to be a temporary prime minister until a new leader is chosen.

Originally all the governor generals came from England. The first Canadian-born person to hold the position was Vincent Massey in 1952. His successor, Georges Philias Vanier, became the first French-Canadian governor general in 1959.

In 1984, Jeanne Sauve was the first and only woman so far to become governor general. She was succeeded by the present governor general, the Right Honorable Ramon Hnatyshyn, who is the 24th person to occupy this position.

Queen Elizabeth II, queen of England and head of the Commonwealth since 1952.

WHO NEEDS THEM?

In a nationwide survey in June 1992, 1,500 Canadians were asked, "Do you think the royal family is good for Canada, bad for Canada, or do you think they make no difference?"

According to the poll, the majority (59%) felt that the royal family made no difference, 27% thought they were good for Canada, 13% felt they were bad for Canada, and 2% were unsure.

THE SENATE

When the Senate was formed in 1867, it had two roles. First, because representation in the House of Commons was according to population size, less populated areas in Canada had their interests safeguarded in a Senate in which the various regions of Canada had equal representation. Second, it reviewed laws passed by the House of Commons. Today, there are 104 members in the Senate— 24 from Ontario, 24 from Quebec, 10 from Nova Scotia, 10 from New Brunswick, six each from Newfoundland, Manitoba, Saskatchewan, Alberta, and British Columbia, four from Prince Edward Island, and one each from the Yukon and Northwest Territories.

Senators are appointed by the governor general, in the queen's name, on the advice

Pierre Trudeau, prime minister of Canada in 1968–79 and 1980–84.

of the prime minister. Before 1965, these appointments were made for life. Today, senators have to retire when they reach 75 years of age. To qualify as a senator, one must be a Canadian citizen, at least 30 years old, own property worth at least $4,000 in the province for which he or she is appointed and be a resident in that province, and have at least another $4,000 of personal property after debts and liabilities. The Senate receives proposed laws in the form of a bill from the House of Commons. It then either passes the bill with or without making changes or amendments to it so that the bill then becomes law, or rejects it.

THE HOUSE OF COMMONS

The House of Commons, as mentioned earlier, is composed of representatives from all parts of the country. These representatives, known as Members of Parliament, are elected by the people to speak on their behalf. They are members of various political parties, under whose banners and policies they run for election.

Because representation in the House is by population, there are now 295 members: 99 from Ontario, 75 from Quebec, 32 from British Columbia, 26 from Alberta, 14 each from Manitoba and Saskatchewan, 11 from Nova Scotia, 10 from New Brunswick, seven from Newfoundland, four from Prince Edward Island, two from the Northwest Territories, and one from the Yukon. Every 10 years, the number of seats for each province is adjusted according to changes in population size.

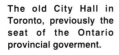

The old City Hall in Toronto, previously the seat of the Ontario provincial goverment.

Once elected, Members of Parliament meet in the House to discuss social, economic, and political issues and to debate and pass laws, a function that the House shares with the Senate.

A third function of the House is to control the finances of the country. This is done through budget and taxation policies.

THE FEDERAL GOVERNMENT Canada's Constitution requires that a new government be formed every five years if not sooner. This is done by the governor general dissolving Parliament, and calling for an election to be held. After the election, the government is formed. The leader of the winning political party is usually appointed prime minister by the governor general. The prime minister then appoints other elected Members of Parliament to form his cabinet. By contrast, the president of the United States and members of his cabinet are not part of either house of Congress.

Usually, each Canadian province is represented by at least one cabinet minister. The cabinet is the policy-forming body of the government. Most cabinet ministers are given areas of responsibility, that is, they are assigned to one or more government departments and are responsible for forming the policies of those departments. The actual work of putting these policies into practice is done by the civil service.

THE OPPOSITION The political party with the second largest number of Members of Parliament forms the official opposition to the government. The leader of this party becomes the leader of Her Majesty's Loyal Opposition. The Opposition performs a very important role in government. It has the responsibility of checking and criticizing government proposals and policies and suggesting ways of improving the governing of the country. It should have sound alternative policies and solutions of its own.

Canada's anthem is O Canada, *and the words are:*

"O Canada, our home and native land,
True patriot love, in all thy sons command.
With glowing hearts we see thee rise,
The True North strong and free.
From far and wide, O Canada, we stand on guard for thee.
God keep our land glorious and free,
O Canada, we stand on guard for thee,
O Canada, we stand on guard for thee."

CANADA'S CONSTITUTION

Canada's Constitution—the set of rules by which the country is governed—goes back to the British North America Act of 1867. It was this Act of the British Parliament that brought about the birth of the new nation of Canada. But because it was an Act of the British Parliament, the Canadian government has had, over the years, to go back to Britain whenever it wanted to amend the Act.

Finally, the British Parliament, at the request of Canada, passed the Canada Act in 1982 that had two great consequences—one was to include in the Canadian Constitution the Constitution Act of 1982, and the other was to transfer all authority to legislate for Canada from Great Britain to Canada.

Today, the Constitution has four main features. Two of these features are as old as the British North America Act of 1867. First, it establishes Canada both as a constitutional monarchy and a parliamentary democracy. Second, it makes Canada a confederation with a division of powers between the federal and provincial levels of government. Of the two new features of the Constitution, the first nationalizes the Constitution and brings it home to Canada. The second is the establishment of the Canadian Charter of Rights and Freedoms.

Parti Québécois leader Jacques Parizeau raises his arms in victory following the massive rejection of the constitutional accord by Canadian voters in October, 1992. The next step could be separation for Quebec, changing the face of Canadian politics forever.

CONSTITUTIONAL CRISIS One might think that after so many years the Constitution is now an established and unshakable fact, but in reality this is not so. When, in November 1981, a historic agreement was reached between the federal government and the nine provincial governments that cleared the way for the proclamation of the Constitution Act of 1982, Quebec withheld its agreement. Since the Act forms the basis of relations between the federal and provincial governments, the entire patriation of the Constitution must depend on an agreement by all provinces. The federal and provincial governments have for many years been trying to agree on such a formula.

In 1987, the ministers met at Meech Lake and produced an accord, but a "no" vote from Manitoba Member of Legislative Assembly Elijah Harper caused it to founder. In 1992, government leaders met again in Charlottetown and drew up a new constitutional agreement. This time, all Canadians were asked in a referendum to vote on the issue, but again the people said "no." To this day Canada's constitutional crisis continues.

THE CHARTER OF RIGHTS AND FREEDOMS

Every Canadian has fundamental rights and freedoms that are guaranteed by the Charter of Rights and Freedoms, as contained in the Constitution Act of 1982.

The Charter, like the American Bill of Rights, guarantees everyone freedom of religion, thought, belief, opinion and expression, including freedom of the press, freedom of peaceful assembly, and freedom of association.

It protects a Canadian citizen's mobility rights (to live, work, and move to wherever he or she chooses), legal rights (to life, liberty, and security), and equality rights (so that it is an offence to discriminate on the basis of race, origin, color, religion, sex, age, or disability).

It recognizes English and French as the two official languages of Canada and guarantees minority language educational rights (that is, a person's right, if in an English- or French-speaking minority, to be taught in his or her own language).

It is important, however, to realize that the Charter expresses basic principles, and that it may be difficult to determine the exact rights of a person in a particular case. It is therefore up to lawyers and judges to reconcile Charter rights and freedoms with the law and with circumstances.

OTTAWA, SEAT OF GOVERNMENT

In the mid-19th century, when Upper and Lower Canada were joined into the United Provinces of Canada, rivalry between the two provinces was such that neither Toronto nor Montreal could serve as the capital. Instead, the legislature had to meet alternately in both cities.

When looking for the site of a new capital, Queen Victoria selected the dull, provincial town of Ottawa (which was formerly known as Bytown, named after Colonel By who constructed the Rideau Canal that cuts through the city) as a compromise because it sat on the border between the two provinces. As Sir Edmund Head, then governor general of Canada, remarked: "I believe that the least objectionable place is the city of Ottawa. Every city is jealous of every other city except Ottawa." It was made the capital of the Dominion of Canada in 1867.

At that time, it had nothing else in its favor. Essayist Goldwin Smith

INDIAN SELF-GOVERNMENT

In 1982, because of the problems caused by the Indian Act and increasing demands by the Indians for more power and a better standard of living, a special committee on Indian self-government was created. In 1983, the committee recommended that the government establish a new relationship with the Indian First Nations, in which self-government was an essential element. Accordingly, the Canadian government has committed itself to seeing that the principle of self-government is entrenched in the Constitution. Regular discussions are being held on exactly how new laws can make possible the handing over of a wide range of powers to the various Indian tribes.

THE ROYAL CANADIAN MOUNTED POLICE

The image of the "Mountie" in his scarlet coat is familiar to all the world as a symbol of Canada. He stands as a beloved symbol of law and order and authority to all Canadians.

When the Canadian government took over control of the vast territories under the Hudson's Bay Company, it realized that something would have to be done to prevent the opening up of the western and northern wilderness from degenerating into the lawlessness that had accompanied much of the opening of the American West.

In 1873, Parliament passed an act establishing a temporary police force for the territories. One hundred and fifty recruits were sent that winter to Fort Garry, followed by another 150 later in the spring. The new police force, named the North-West Mounted Police, was organized along the lines of a cavalry regiment, armed with guns and dressed much like soldiers in a scarlet tunic and blue trousers to stress their symbolic link with the British army. The new force set up a network of police posts and patrolled the land, effectively curbing the lawlessness of adventurers, many of whom had come from the south. When gold was discovered in the Klondike, the North-West Mounted Police was immediately sent into the Yukon. Its presence ensured that the Klondike gold rush was the most orderly in history.

By the early 20th century, Canadians had begun to recognize that the mounted police were here to stay. The Canadian government decided in 1919 to expand the Royal North-West Mounted Police, as it was by then known, into a national police force. When the legislation took effect in 1920, it moved its headquarters from Ottawa to Regina. It became known as the Royal Canadian Mounted Police and gradually took over policing duties all over the country.

Today, a member of the RCMP looks very much like any other police officer in a blue uniform. The scarlet tunic, the image of the "Mountie" as popularized in books and movies, can be seen only on ceremonial occasions and in pictures on tourist and other promotional brochures.

called it, "A sub-Arctic lumber village, converted by royal mandate into a political cockpit." Today, however, Ottawa has lived up to its role as the seat of government. It has a population of over 303,000. It is a modern city situated at the confluence of three rivers, a beautiful setting which has been enhanced by the National Capital Commission whose work is to improve the city with features such as beautiful parks and sidewalks lined with flowers.

ECONOMY

CANADA'S RICH NATURAL RESOURCES have from the earliest times provided food, shelter, and clothing for its people. It was Canada's natural wealth that attracted the first European settlers and traders who came and worked the land. Canada's natural resources have always been the backbone of its economy, although the economy is becoming increasingly diversified and industrialized.

AGRICULTURE

In the early days, most Canadians were farmers. The market for their produce was domestic, and there was a lot of subsistence farming. This picture has changed drastically. In 1986, only 3% of all Canadians lived on farms. Despite this low percentage, the average farm is much larger in size and produces much more because of technological advances.

Just over half of what Canada produces is exported to other countries. The importance of agriculture to the Canadian economy is reflected in the help that farmers get from the government. There are many programs to regulate and promote agriculture and improve education

Above: **Grain storage in Manitoba.**

Opposite: **Logger and Logs being transported downriver. The forestry industry is one of Canada's most important industries.**

and research in the subject. Canadian farmers raise livestock—traditionally, beef and dairy cattle, pigs, and poultry—grow grain, and produce special crops like fruit and vegetables and forest products.

The prairie regions of Manitoba, Saskatchewan, and Alberta contain almost all of the farmland in Canada, producing grain crops and supporting a large beef cattle industry. Saskatchewan produces much of Canada's wheat, and Alberta is the chief producer of feed-grain and beef cattle. Potatoes are the main crop in Prince Edward Island; Quebec is the world's largest producer of maple syrup.

Forestry products provide Canada with a highly lucrative source of income.

FORESTRY

About 10% of the world's total forest area (about 2.13 million square miles of mainly coniferous trees) is found in Canada. As a result, Canada is the world's leading exporter of forest products.

The forest industry includes logging and paper and pulp mills. It is concentrated in the provinces of British Columbia, Quebec, and Ontario. The wood and paper industries produce a wide range of products—from basic lumber, plywood, and paper to completed, manufactured products such as prefabricated buildings and furniture. Canada exports most of these products, mainly to the United States.

FOREST MANAGEMENT An important part of the forestry industry is the protection of forests. Almost as many trees are destroyed each year by fire, pests, and disease as are harvested commercially. Provincial forestry agencies are responsible for seeing that the loss of trees is reduced. Thus, thinning, pruning, and clearing of forests is part of provincial forest management.

Reforestation, or the replanting of trees, is another important part of forest management. Millions of trees are replanted each year to ensure that the forest is a renewable resource.

Despite the existence of forest management, the logging of forests is a very controversial subject as the forest is home to a large number of animals and plants and has a direct effect on the world's climate. The forest industry faces a great deal of opposition from conservationists and environmentalists.

FISHING

Bordered on three sides by water, and with thousands of rivers and lakes, it is hardly surprising that Canada is the world's second largest exporter of fish products. In 1989, Canada exported three-quarters of its fish production, worth $1.92 billion. Half of this went to the United States, followed by Japan and the European Community.

Lobster traps on a pier side in Nova Scotia, one of Canada's primary fishing regions.

The main exports were cod, herring, crabs, lobsters, and scallops from the Atlantic Coast, and halibut and salmon from the Pacific Coast. Fishing is the main industry in many parts of Atlantic Canada, with the provinces of Newfoundland and Nova Scotia accounting for 80% of the region's total catch. British Columbia has the largest commercial fishery in the country, catching mainly salmon.

The federal government is responsible for the management of fisheries in the ocean and in national parks; provincial governments manage the freshwater fisheries within their boundaries. The federal government has had to impose severe restrictions on cod fishing off the coast of Newfoundland as a result of domestic and foreign over-fishing.

THE CANADIAN COW

The cow was an early "settler" of Canada, coming over from France with explorer Jacques Cartier on his first voyage to Canada in 1534. In 1606, more cows were imported, and in 1610, they were shipped to New France by Samuel de Champlain. When the United Empire Loyalists fled New England for New Brunswick in the period 1778–1785, they too brought cattle with them. The Hudson's Bay Company also helped ship cattle from England to the Red River settlement. In the west, the company shipped cattle from California to British Columbia.

Potash miner in Saskatoon, Saskatchewan.

MINING

Canada produces over 60 different mineral products, making the mining industry a major factor in the country's economic development.

In terms of volume, Canada is the world's largest exporter of minerals. It leads the world in the export of uranium and zinc; it is second in nickel, asbestos, gypsum, potash, elemental sulphur, and titanium; and it is one of the top five producers of aluminum, cadmium, cobalt, copper, gold, lead, silver, and platinum.

About 80% of what is produced is exported to the United States, Japan, and the European Community. With the exception of just a few minerals, Canada is able to meet its own domestic mineral needs.

The provinces own all the natural resources that are within their boundaries and control the exploration, development, conservation, and production of these minerals. To ensure a supply of metals and minerals, the mining industry continues to explore and map mineral deposits and other geological features and develop new mining methods and equipment.

THE GOLD RUSH

In 1848, two tough gold prospectors, McDaniels and Adams, discovered a large quantity of gold dust at the Fraser and Thompson rivers that have their source in the Cariboo Mountains of British Columbia. When news of the Fraser River gold spread south, about 25,000 miners from California, Washington, Oregon, Latin America, and Hawaii rushed north. At the height of the Fraser River gold rush, about 10,000 miners were spread out over a 200-mile area. Mining the Fraser was difficult. Melting snows engorged the river and mining could not take place until August when the river was at its summer low. In winter, the freezing cold and deep snows made mining dangerous and often impossible. In 1862, an even bigger gold rush began when hopeful adventurers, following the Fraser River north, hit the jackpot at William's Creek, in the Cariboo region.

Many made their fortune, and no doubt squandered it just as quickly, but the real benefits of the Fraser and Cariboo gold rushes were the blossoming of the town of Victoria into a busy city and the opening up of the interior of British Columbia.

In 1896, gold was discovered in the Klondike by a prospector, George Washington Carmack, and his two companions, Skookum Jim and Tagish Charlie. The Klondike was Canada's greatest gold rush. It lasted a few spectacular years, from 1897 to 1900, during which $40 million in gold was mined in the area. Conditions were harsh—the frozen ground had to be thawed out with wood fires before it could be dug and the gold-bearing rock brought out. But that did not stop gold fever from infecting the thousands who flocked to the Klondike from all points of the globe. Dawson City grew into a boom town. At the height of the rush, it had a population of about 30,000 people. Today, there are only about 1,700 residents.

ENERGY RESOURCES

Most of Canada's energy comes from crude oil, natural gas, coal, nuclear power, and hydroelectricity. A small amount comes from sources such as bio-energy (energy from plant or animal material such as forestry and wood processing residue, crop remains, and animal waste), solar, and wind energy.

As an industrialized country, Canada consumes a large portion of its energy output. Nevertheless, it is still able to export energy, sending over 80% of its petroleum, natural gas, and electricity south to the United States.

Wood, which used to be the main source of the country's energy, is still popular. This is especially so in the country. Wood wastes and wood chips are another source of fuel for heating.

Canada has abundant coal reserves. Mined as early as 1639, it accounts for 14% of Canada's energy supply and produces 17% of Canada's electricity. The provinces of Alberta, Saskatchewan, and Nova Scotia are almost completely dependent on coal for their electricity. Canada exports coal to the Pacific Rim countries, Europe, and South America.

The Irving pulp mill in Saint John, New Brunswick.

More recently, oil and gas have become the main energy sources in Canada and the world. Canada is the world's third largest producer of natural gas and the ninth largest producer of crude oil. It was only in 1947 that oil was first discovered in the country, in Leduc, Alberta. By 1987, 168,000 oil wells had been drilled in Canada.

Canada is the world's leading producer of hydroelectricity. It has major hydroelectric projects in Newfoundland, Quebec, Manitoba, and British Columbia.

FREE TRADE AGREEMENTS

In 1988, Canada and the United States signed a free trade agreement, providing both countries with a mechanism to work out any trade disputes that may arise in a fair and efficient manner. For the individual traveler, the Free Trade Agreement reduces or eliminates customs duty on all goods of United States and Canadian origin purchased for personal use. While some goods such as calculators, computers, skates, and skis became duty free immediately, duties on other consumer items such as furniture, small appliances, video games, clothing, linen, and tobacco will be reduced over the next five to 10 years.

Vancouver harbor is a major point of exit for resource-rich British Columbia's export trade.

During 1989–1991, Canadian merchandise exports to the United States grew by almost 11% to $260 billion (US), a result that the Canadian government says is due to the Free Trade Agreement.

In 1992, the leaders of Canada, the United States, and Mexico signed the North American Free Trade Agreement, which will create the world's biggest and richest free-trade market. Mexico is Canada's largest trading partner in Latin America, with two-way trade exceeding $2.4 billion in 1991. As with the FTA, the NAFTA will gradually eliminate import duties that restrict trade and investment among the three countries.

Nevertheless, not everyone believes that the trade agreements are good for the Canadian economy. Opponents of these agreements fear that it will lead to a loss in jobs, business failures, and a flooding of the Canadian market with cheap goods made with cheap labor.

THE CANADIAN WORKER

At the time of the Canadian Confederation, almost half of Canadian workers farmed the land. But, by 1989, the number of farm workers had dropped to 3% of the Canadian labor force, while only 2% were employed in other primary industries.

A construction worker in Quebec.

By contrast, there were more Canadian workers in the service sector (33%), trade (18%), manufacturing (17%), and transportation, communication, and other utilities (8%). Government workers formed 7% of the total work force, while construction, finance, insurance, and real estate employed 6% each.

Since 1969, increasingly more women have joined the labor force. In 1989, women made up 44% of the working population.

The average income of Canadian families rose from $19,700 in 1979 to $40,000 in 1989.

WORK CONDITIONS

The Canadian worker has come a long way since the days when the economy was more farm-oriented than industrial, but this has not happened without a struggle. Towards the end of the 19th century, the Royal Commission on the Relations of Labor and Capital in Canada revealed the hardships of the working class—people worked long hours, children too had to go to work, wages were poor and made even worse when money could be deducted as fines for perceived misconduct.

TRADE UNION HISTORY

The first Canadian unions were craft unions, uniting skilled workers such as printers, carpenters, painters, bakers, and tailors. But unions were considered illegal until 1872, when a showdown between printers in Toronto campaigning for a nine-hour working day (instead of their 10-hour day) clashed with the publishers. Following a mass protest in front of the legislative buildings in Queen's Park in Toronto, the Canadian Parliament passed the Trade Union Act, legalizing unions.

Another landmark in trade union history occurred when workers realized that they could have greater power if they formed a national organization. In 1886, the craft unions formed the Trades and Labor Congress of Canada (TLC). In 1902, the TLC joined the American Federation of Labor (AFL).

Meanwhile, other unions were forming. Unskilled workers, unable to join the craft unions, formed industrial unions of their own, often with the help of American unionists who came north to help organize Canadian workers. In 1927, they banded together to form the All-Canadian Congress of Labor (ACCL). In 1940, the ACCL linked up with the Congress of Industrial Organizations (CIO) in the United States and became the Canadian Congress of Labor (CCL).

Much trouble accompanied these early years of union activity, especially in the years after World War II—strikes were frequent and often violent, with unions fighting employers, police, and the government. But out of this turmoil came cohesion. The craft unions and industrial unions, together with several other national unions, joined together in 1956 to form the Canadian Labor Congress. Today, the CLC represents more than two million workers in Canada.

Today, workers are protected by labor laws. The Canadian Labor Code, which regulates federal jobs, is a measure of what a worker in Canada can expect. Among other things, the code limits the maximum working day to eight hours and the maximum working week to 40 hours. Generally, no more than eight hours of overtime is permitted per week, and overtime pay must be at least one and a half times the regular rate.

The minimum wage paid for any kind of work is frequently reviewed and adjusted to take into account the state of the economy and the effects of inflation.

Employers must give their employees an annual paid vacation, the minimum being two weeks a year. In addition, a human rights code prohibits job discrimination on the basis of race, religion, national origin, color, sex, age, or marital status.

CANADIANS

THE MAKING OF CANADA is a story of struggle, not so much of wars and bloodshed, but of the struggle of men and women who had to learn to live in a harsh, hostile, and unforgiving land.

Confederation united the French and the English into an uneasy alliance. Since then, there has been an almost constant flow of immigrants from all over the world in search of a better life. Canada has provided them all with the opportunity to turn this dream into reality.

ROOM TO BREATHE

Canada is the world's second largest country and ranks as one of the richest. Despite a history of immigration, it is still one of the most thinly populated countries in the world, ranked 31st in terms of population size. The 27 million people living in Canada are not evenly spread out across the 10 provinces and two territories.

Much of the north remains largely inhospitable, so that two out of three people live within 125 miles of Canada's border with the United States, with 62% of the population concentrated in the two provinces of Ontario and Quebec. Most Canadians now live in cities.

Opposite: **Inuit woman in the Northwest Territories.**

Below: **Two boys in Sydney, Nova Scotia.**

Chinatown in Vancouver. A visible example of Canada's cosmopolitan make-up.

THEY CAME, THEY SAW, THEY STAYED

Immigration has played an important part in the making of Canada. At the time of Confederation, the population was made up of the descendants of European immigrants, American Loyalists, and the native people.

English and French were followed by Scottish, German, and Swiss immigrants who settled in Nova Scotia. During the American Revolution (1775–1783), about 50,000 Protestant Loyalists left America and settled in the Atlantic provinces and Ontario to avoid being a part of the new American republic. The great potato famine in Ireland in the mid-19th century brought tens of thousands of Irish settlers.

Asians were also an integral part of the early history of immigration in Canada. Poverty was usually the reason many Chinese, Japanese, Pakistanis, and East Indians left their homelands. Many Japanese also emigrated to escape serving in the army when military conscription was introduced in Japan in 1873.

At the turn of the century came the big government push to populate the huge and empty prairie lands that lay between the two coasts. Through a massive publicity campaign Europeans, then beset by poverty, overcrowded land, persecution, and other troubles, were lured across the sea by the promise of free land—all they had to do was to clear it, farm it, and make it their home. From 1910 to 1914, about 3 million settlers flooded into Canada.

A SAFE HAVEN

Since World War II, Canada has experienced another period of population growth that was first fueled by a "baby boom" and then by increased immigration.

Tens of thousands of immigrants from eastern and southern Europe, previously considered undesirable, were admitted. In addition, Canada took in many Ugandan, Chilean, Hungarian, Czechoslovakian, and Southeast Asian refugees. By the 1970s, the country had become known as a land of opportunity and was a magnet for people everywhere who were seeking a better life. This

Today's Canada is a multicultural and multi-racial society where all creeds and colors are accepted.

created a trend that has persisted to this day. People facing an uncertain or troubled future in their home countries continue to look to Canada as a haven.

In 1978, a new Immigration Act was proclaimed that forms the basis of Canada's immigration policy today. It takes into consideration the state of the country's population, economy, society, and culture, while helping families to reunite. It does not discriminate on racial and ethnic grounds, and recognizes Canada's obligation as one of the world's most favored countries to help refugees of all kinds. This does not mean that immigrants to Canada have very few problems when it comes to integrating with the existing, and still predominantly British, society (except in Quebec where the French-speaking population dominates).

FIRST PEOPLES TODAY

This Inuit woman is involved in the traditional activity of hide preparation.

It has often been said that there are two founding peoples in Canada, the French and the British. But today, the idea that there were actually three founding peoples—the native Indians, the French, and the British—is gaining precedence.

Anthropologists estimate that there were about 350,000 native people at the time of the arrival of the Europeans. For many decades after the Europeans came, the native population declined due to disease, starvation, and warfare, and the existence of their unique cultures was threatened.

At the time of Confederation, there were between 100,000 and 125,000 Indians in Canada. But by the 1940s, the Indians began to assert themselves, and today, there are more than 750,000 Indians. The Indian population continues to increase at a faster rate than the rest of the population.

Most of them live in communities called "Indian bands" on reservations that have been set aside for their exclusive use. There are 598 Indian bands on 2,284 reservations and Crown land. The bands vary in size. The smallest in 1980 was a band in New Westminster, British Columbia, with only two members. The largest band is the Six Nations of the Grand River in Ontario, which has about 16,000 members.

Socially and economically, the Indians are generally poorer than other Canadians due to the discrimination they suffered in the early years. But these conditions are improving. Close to half of all Indians on reservations depend on social assistance from the government. The unemployment rate among Indians is more than three times that for all Canadians, although one must remember this number includes many Indians who continue with their traditional activities of hunting and fishing.

In 1965, fewer than half of the houses on Indian reservations had electricity, and even fewer had proper water and sewerage systems—services which the rest of the country took for granted. By 1989, however, most houses on the reservations had running water, sewers, or septic tanks.

With improving conditions, Indians are slowly making the government and other Canadians aware that they were once free, self-sustaining people. Today, councils put in place by the Indians manage almost all Indian affairs. More Indian children attend schools that are operated by the bands as well as government schools. There are more than 5,000 active Indian businesses. Many of these were set up with financial help from the government.

Indians are seeking their own forms of self-government. By so doing, they hope to assume their proper place in Canadian society, and at the same time maintain the rich diversity of their traditional cultures that evolved over thousands of years before European contact.

Indian girl in traditional costume.

NOT ALL WERE EQUAL

Not all of those who came found that they were welcomed with open arms by Canadian society, which was largely white, Protestant, and of English stock. English, Scottish, and American immigrants were officially encouraged to come, as they would fit best into the established community. Even the Irish, who could be considered Canada's first huge influx of foreigners, though white and English-speaking, did not quite fit in as they were Roman Catholics and held different social and cultural values.

When the immigrants came, many of them gravitated to the cities instead of remaining in the isolation of the country. They provided the cheap labor needed in the factories and worked in the mines and lumberyards.

Many Canadians did not like their presence, necessary though it was, and racist immigration laws were enforced. For example, several anti-Chinese laws were passed, first imposing a "head tax" of $40 on every Chinese entering the country (this was finally raised to $400) and culminating in the Chinese Immigration Act of 1923 that prohibited any more Chinese from entering Canada. It took 24 years before that Act was repealed. Those already in the country were denied their citizenship rights and not allowed to vote.

During World War II, all Japanese who lived within a 100-mile band along the Pacific coast were taken inland because their loyalty to Canada was suspect.

Unlike in the United States, Africans do not have much of a presence in Canada. The reason for this is that they were deliberately kept out of the country. During the great flood of immigrants into the country before World War I, many African-Americans planned to emigrate north. But a public outcry led to a government move to reject them, should they turn up at the border, as "unfit for admission on medical grounds."

In traditional costumes, members of the Kingston German Society in Ontario meet to celebrate their heritage.

MULTICULTURALISM

The United States is thought of as a "melting pot," in which many different ingredients blend into a new ethnic and cultural group that is American society. Canada, on the other hand, is often called a "mosaic," that is, the sum of all the different ethnic and cultural groups where each group retains its distinctive characteristics.

Multiculturalism is the policy that arises from this mosaic. It is the policy of Canada "to recognize all Canadians as full and equal participants in Canadian society." The federal Department of State and the provincial departments of Citizenship and Social Services issue publications and have many services to help newcomers to the country.

PREFERRED IMMIGRANTS

Even when the government was actively recruiting prospective immigrants, it had a scale of preferences. British and American settlers were "preferred," followed by French, Belgians, Dutch, Scandinavians, Swiss, Finns, Russians, Austro-Hungarians, Germans, Ukrainians, and Poles. Italians, Slavs, Greeks, and Syrians were less desirable, while Jews, Asians, and Africans were at the very bottom of the list.

THE CANADIAN IDENTITY

Think of a Canadian, and several stock images may come to mind—the lumberjack, a Mountie, or someone who is bilingual in French and English and lives in a land covered with snow and ice.

The casual observer may find it hard to tell the difference between a Canadian and an American—they dress alike, talk almost alike, and have a similar lifestyle. But Canadians also stereotype themselves—they call themselves dull, boring, introverted, cautious, given to compromise and negotiation. Above all, they know they are "not Americans."

In a country that is made up of immigrants from many lands, it is not easy to pin down the Canadian identity, and this is a problem that seems to have provoked a seemingly endless discussion among Canadians in order to answer the question: "Who are we?"

Canadians are a relaxed, easy-going people.

Perhaps another reason for this is that Canadian history is remarkably free of bloodshed, war, or revolution, such as often attends the birth of many nations. Canada cut its ties with Britain in a slow and hesitant manner. It took almost a century after Confederation before Canadians recognized themselves as being Canadians, noted Canadian historian George Woodcock.

In addition, the United States has always had a strong influence on its northern neighbor. Internationally, Canada has always seemed to be the weaker, smaller, and poorer cousin, often following America's political lead and seldom striking out on its own. Culturally, Canadians not only looked south of the border for direction, but they went south too, for it was difficult for a Canadian to gain recognition in Canada without first having made a name for himself or herself in the United States. Artists, writers, journalists, and actors crossed the border to where the opportunities were. It has been only recently that Canadiana—all things Canadian—has been given the attention it deserves. Perhaps the key to the question of Canadian identity lies not so much in what similarities there are, but in those qualities that set them apart from others. History, geography, and climate have all contributed in shaping the Canadian.

ON CANADIANS AND THEIR IDENTITY

"I know the worth of this unprecedented idea, the idea of unity without uniformity which is the distinctive mark of Canada, the stamp of Canadian identity."—Duff Roblin, premier of Manitoba in the 1960s.

"We moved from British influence to American influence without much feeling of purely national identity in between."—Lester B. Pearson, Prime Minister of Canada 1963–1968.

"I think our identity will have to be something which is partly British, partly French, partly American, partly derived from a variety of other influences which are too numerous even to catalogue."—Eugene Forsey, Senator.

"Dull and introverted and all the rest of it though we may be, Canadians have as a people a national gift for tolerance and an acquired skill at compromise."—Richard Gwyn, newspaper columnist.

"The problem is that Canada is not so much a nation, more an act of faith ... I asked dozens of people what made them specifically Canadian and every single one defined their country purely in terms of not being American."—Simon Hoggart, journalist.

"... we have our own distinct identity and our own way of doing things and that part of that identity is our tendency to constant self-examination."—Pierre Berton, writer.

LIFESTYLE

CONTRARY TO THE BELIEF, held especially by people who are not North Americans, that family values and family life are in danger of vanishing in North America, the institution of the family is alive and well. In 1986, four out of five Canadians lived as part of a family unit. Nevertheless, the pressures of modern living have had an impact on the family structure. A longer life expectancy has changed the demographic picture. Society has had to cope with more older people and their needs. At the same time, the ability to move quickly and easily from one part of the country to another has led to young Canadians moving out of their family homes to work in other towns and provinces.

FAMILY LIFE

The average Canadian family is getting smaller. People are getting married later in life and are not having as many children as the previous generation. There is also an increasing tendency for younger, single members of the family to leave home and make their lives and careers away from the town or province where they grew up. Other factors are the increase in families in which there is only one parent and the fact that more unmarried women are having children.

One form of family that has made its appearance only since World War II and seems to be growing in number is the family in which the adults are not married but have decided to live together and form a family unit. This is known as a common-law union and is found especially among younger Canadians and those who have been divorced. Nevertheless, many common-law unions do end in marriage.

Divorce is also increasing, ever since 1968 when Canada changed the law and made it easier for couples to get a divorce. By the mid-1980s, almost half of all marriages had ended in divorce.

"Yes, Alec, it is I, your father, speaking." And with these words, the first message was transmitted by long-distance telephone from Melville Bell who was in Brantford, Ontario, to his son, Alexander Graham Bell, eight miles away in Paris, Ontario, in 1876. Since then, Canadians have not stopped talking on the telephone.

Opposite: **Because of the extent and variety of Canada's wilderness, camping has always been a favorite pastime.**

Preschool children on an outing.

THE GROWING-UP YEARS

Today, in many families both parents work. Many young Canadian children therefore have experienced being placed in the care of someone other than their parents. The care-giver may be another mother who looks after several children in her home, or it may be a teacher at a day-care center.

By the time they are five or six years old, most children have started school. By Canadian law, children must attend school between the ages of six and 15 or 16.

School usually begins with two kindergarten years and finishes in either 11th or 12th grade. Elementary school generally covers the years from kindergarten to sixth grade, junior high school is generally seventh to eighth or ninth grades, and senior high school is from 10th to 11th or 12th grades.

After graduation from 12th grade, students find a job or continue their formal education at community colleges, technical institutes, or universities. In some provinces, like Ontario and Quebec, students who wish to enter a university after 11th or 12th grade must complete one or two more years of senior high school. The University of Toronto, University of British Columbia, and McGill University in Montreal are three well known universities.

Canadian children mature and learn to be independent at an early age. Boys and girls learn to socialize with the opposite sex from an early age because most Canadian schools are coeducational. How to be attractive and popular in school, dating, and going steady are concerns that come early in the life of the adolescent Canadian. Sex education is a part of the school curriculum. Increased social and educational pressures can make the young susceptible to the lure of drugs and alcohol, or other problems.

Many young Canadians are introduced to working life even while they are still in school. Doing the occasional odd job—cleaning yards, washing cars, mowing lawns—or holding a part-time job, such as having a paper route, is not uncommon. They leave home almost immediately after school, either to go to college or a university or to a job that may take them out of their home town.

TEEN VALUES

In a survey of 4,000 teenagers conducted by sociologist Reg Bibby in 1992, Canadian teenagers were found to be increasingly more individualistic, placing emphasis on their rights and freedom to pursue their own lifestyles. Bibby and co-author Don Posterski published their findings in a book called *Teen Trends: A Nation in Motion*.

"They care about justice and equality and the environment. They're optimistic about the future. Their self-esteem is high. They're increasingly saying 'no' to drugs. And their happiness level exceeds that of teenagers of the '50s and '60s, the so-called Happy Days era," Bibby said in a newspaper interview. Unfortunately, the proportion of youths has fallen who believe that values like honesty, politeness, and hard work are very important.

GROWING OLD IN CANADA

Canadians have one of the highest life expectancies in the world. A Canadian woman can now expect to live for almost 80 years, while Canadian men can expect to live for about 73 years. This, coupled with the fact that people are waiting longer to have children and then choosing to have fewer children than the generation before them, has resulted in a population with a greater proportion of older people.

The elderly population is growing more rapidly than any other age group in the country. When a Canadian grows old, his or her life is far from

Boating with the grandchildren. Whatever the age, Canadians love the outdoors.

over. Often it just takes a new turn. Released from the need to work, retired people find other pursuits to occupy their time. They join choirs, form musical and theatrical groups, go hiking, learn new hobbies, or even go back to school. Many of them volunteer their skills and services both in Canada and overseas. Marriages between senior Canadians who are 65 years old or older are common.

The importance of this segment of Canadian society can be seen in the social infrastructure and facilities that cater to the needs of the elderly. Businesses recognize that there is a lot of money to be gained from these senior citizens. Older people get discount days in stores, travel for less, and enjoy lower fees for services.

"Senior" centers have been developed in every province. These are multi-purpose centers that provide community social services to the elderly. They offer all kinds of recreational, cultural, and educational activities. Housing developers build apartments and condominiums that are sold or rented exclusively to older people.

A WELFARE STATE

In contrast to the United States, Canada can be considered a welfare state. The government has many health and social welfare programs such as the Child Tax Credit, Medicare, Canada Pension Plan, Canada Assistance Plan, and a Guaranteed Income Supplement. This is to ensure the well-being of all Canadians. Depending on the kind of government that comes to power, whether liberal or socialist in outlook, these social programs may either be cut back to reduce the financial burden they place on the government or increased to be compatible with the social philosophy of reducing inequality in society.

This couple can expect to be cared for the whole of their lives under Canada's welfare system.

Low-income families with children under the age of 18 receive monthly payments from the government, called child tax benefits, to help them with the financial cost of raising these children.

Canada's nationwide health insurance system is designed to ensure that everyone in the country receives medical care and treatment when they require it and that no one is denied access because they are too poor to afford it. The provinces and territories organize and finance their own health insurance plans; the federal government contributes to it. People pay toward the plan, but the amount they pay varies according to their income level. They are not charged directly when they visit a doctor or are hospitalized.

Both employers and employees make contributions to the Canada Pension Plan, which then provides a pension to workers and their families when they are retired.

Unemployment insurance is a nationwide program that helps people who are out of work.

WOMEN IN CANADA

The organized women's movement in Canada developed in the late 19th century, focusing mainly on gaining voting rights for women, access to higher education, and equality in the workplace.

In the late 1960s, the women's movement took hold of much of the Western world. In Canada, the majority of married women had a paying job outside the home.

In the late 1970s, women's organizations pointed to the fact that women and children were being abused by men in their own family. This led to a law which permits intervention in cases of domestic assault. Women were also successful in getting the principle of sexual equality incorporated in the Charter of Rights and Freedoms that formed a part of the Canadian Constitution of 1982.

Despite the advances that have been made with regard to the status of women in society, the fact still remains that even today the majority of women generally hold two jobs—a low-paid job in the labor force and an unpaid job at home. While women make up an increasing proportion of the workforce, they still tend to be paid less than men.

Many women are now aware that they have the right to independence and to control their own lives. They join unions and other organizations that aim to establish equal pay for equal work, maternity leave and benefits, adequate daycare facilities, the end of discrimination in the work place, and protection against sexual harassment.

Today, Canadian women have gained equality in many respects, and continue to raise the consciousness of society with regard to the rights of women.

MILESTONES FOR CANADIAN WOMEN

- In 1867, Emily Stowe became the first Canadian woman with a medical degree to practice medicine in Canada. But she was forced to study for her degree at the New York Medical College for women because women were not allowed into medical schools in Canada.

- In 1872, married women in Ontario were allowed to own property. British Columbia passed a similar law later that year.

- In 1883, Emily Stowe's daughter, Augusta, became the first woman to earn a medical degree in Canada. She studied at the Toronto School of Medicine.

- In 1897, Clara Brett Martin became the first woman lawyer in Canada and the British Empire.

- In 1916, after a long campaign, women in Manitoba, Alberta, and Saskatchewan gained the right to vote. Women in Ontario and British Columbia were allowed to vote the following year.

- In 1921, Agnes MacPhail became the first woman Member of Parliament.

- In 1951, Charlotte Whitton became mayor of Ottawa, the first woman to become mayor of a large city.

- In 1960, the Canadian Bill of Rights was passed forbidding any kind of discrimination based on sex.

- In 1971, the Canada Labor Code was amended to provide women with a maternity leave of 17 weeks. The Code also prohibited discrimination in the work place on grounds of sex or marital status.

- In 1980, Jeanne Sauve became the first woman Speaker of the House of Commons.

- In 1983, Roberta Bondar became the first Canadian woman to become an astronaut. She was one of six scientists chosen as Canada's original astronauts.

- In 1985, the Indian Act was amended to restore status to Indian women who had lost this status by marrying a non-Indian.

- In 1989, Audrey McLaughlin became the first woman to head a major political party in North America, the New Democratic Party.

- In 1991, Rita Johnston became British Columbia's prime minister, the first woman in Canada to become premier.

Traffic in downtown Toronto, Ontario.

PEOPLE ON THE MOVE

Canada is such a big country that from its earliest days how to get from one place to another has been an important aspect of Canadian life. The country owes its unity to the railway, which overcame muskeg (bogs), swamps, and mountain ranges to link Pacific coast with Atlantic coast.

There are two major railways in Canada: the Canadian Pacific Railway and the Canadian National Railway, plus several smaller ones.

Passenger rail service is provided by a government company called VIA Rail, but people usually drive, take inter-city bus services, or travel by air when traveling long distances. As a result, VIA Rail has had to cut back on its services, and railway tracks are being pulled up in many parts of the country. Even so, one can still travel by rail from west to east, from Vancouver across the Rocky Mountains to Edmonton, Winnipeg, and Toronto, on VIA Rail's Western Transcontinental service.

Major international airports in Toronto, Vancouver, Calgary, and Montreal link Canada with the rest of the world. There are also many large and small airports throughout the country that cater to domestic travel. Canada's two main international airlines are Air Canada and Canadian Airlines. Other smaller air carriers offer air links with most of the communities across the country. They are especially important to the small, remote communities in the north, which get most of their services by air.

Most important is the network of roads that crisscross Canada. Roads of all kinds, from logging road to multilane highway, ensure that people and goods can travel to almost every part of the country. The Trans-Canada

THE ALASKA HIGHWAY

The first roads were built for military reasons and one prime example of this was the Alaska Highway. When the Japanese attacked Pearl Harbor in 1941, the United States was forced to consider building an inland route to Alaska that would be less vulnerable to Japanese air attack. The highway, which was built in 1942 by 11,000 American soldiers and thousands more Canadian and American civilians, now stretches 1,388 miles from Dawson Creek, British Columbia, to Delta Junction near Fairbanks, Alaska. Almost all of this surface is now asphalt. Soldiers working from both north and south took eight months to finally meet near Kluane Lake in southwestern Yukon and complete the road.

Highway can be considered Canada's national highway—it is 4,900 miles long and took more than half a century to complete. It stretches from St. John's in Newfoundland to Victoria in British Columbia.

In 1988, there were more than 12 million passenger cars in Canada. Owning a car is not a luxury in Canada; it is necessary for work, shopping, and recreation. Many households own more than one vehicle—both parents often have their own cars to take them to their different places of work, and when the children reach the age of 16, they are ready to learn to drive and to have their own set of wheels.

Even when they are not on the move, Canadians are often covering the miles by telephone. The Canadian love for the telephone began with its invention by Alexander Graham Bell, himself a Canadian, in 1876. Almost every home has a telephone, often with more than one extension. Cordless phones, teen phones, answering machines, and facsimile machines are all part and parcel of life in Canada today.

Waiting for the bus. Buses are one of the many ways Canadians get around in their cities.

COUNTRY MOUSE AND CITY MOUSE

Since the 19th century, Canadians have disdained the rural life and gravitated toward urban centers. Over three-quarters live in an urban environment. The percentage of urban population varies from province to province. In Ontario, British Columbia, and Alberta today, most of the population is urban. But in other parts of Canada, such as in the Atlantic provinces, many people still live in small towns and villages. In Prince Edward Island the majority of the population is still rural.

Canada's cities, like cities elsewhere, have a central downtown area dominated by business activities. Around this core are residential communities with their own infrastructure of shopping centers, businesses, and services.

Life in the big city is exciting, and entertainment is available day and night. But the hustle and bustle of city living and the crowds bring problems of increasing violence, racial tension, pollution, and stress. It is increasingly unsafe to walk city streets at night for fear of being robbed, assaulted, or killed.

Relaxing and having a drink in Vancouver, British Columbia.

Many small towns owe their existence to a single industry that is the major employer. Thus there are logging towns, mining towns, and fishing villages. They range from small settlements of a hundred or so residents to towns and villages of a few thousand. Some small settlements are so remote, their only link with the rest of the country is by chartered planes.

CLOSING THE LOOP

Reduce, reuse, and recycle are the three "Rs" of the 1990s. Many municipalities and environmentally-conscious groups are encouraging people to reduce the amount of garbage they take to the dump, by trying to reuse anything they can or recycling what they cannot. Recyclable items, such as plastics, newspapers, metal cans, and cardboard, are brought to collection centers. They are sorted and sold to manufacturers who turn plastics, paper, glass, and metals back into new products that end up back on the supermarket shelf, thus closing the loop. Many big stores, especially supermarkets, collect used plastic and brown paper shopping bags right in their stores for the same purpose.

CARING FOR THE ENVIRONMENT

Canadians, like so many other people in developed countries, are great consumers. At the local garbage dump, paper products—newspapers, packaging, telephone books, mail-order catalogues, and advertising flyers—make up about half the volume of trash thrown away. Plastics, in the form of packaging, bottles, appliances, construction materials, and so on, make up about a quarter of all garbage. In fact, Canadians consume about 170 lbs per person of plastic products a year. Add to this the pollution that comes from industrial waste and a lifestyle in which two cars per family is the norm, and the impression one gets is that Canadians are a wasteful, uncaring people.

But this picture is becoming less true as more people are beginning to understand that they have to take care of the environment for the sake of themselves and for future generations. There is no doubt that Canadians are becoming more environmentally conscious. Features in newspapers, magazines, and on television increasingly focus on how one can learn to care for the environment, reduce the effects of acid rain, and focus attention on disappearing forests and wildlife.

Though pollution is common in Canada, Canadians are becoming increasingly aware of environmental concerns.

RELIGION

CANADA'S HISTORY has been inextricably bound up with religion from its earliest times. The native people of Canada were filled with the spirit of the land and a reverence for nature and creation. When the French explorers came, they brought with them missionaries who introduced Christianity to the natives.

In later years, Canada became a refuge for many people suffering from religious persecution in their own lands. They came here to practice their own faiths in peace. The early immigrants were followed by millions of others who introduced even more diversity into the religious fabric of the country. Freedom to practice one's own religion is entrenched in and protected by the Charter of Rights and Freedoms.

NATIVE BELIEFS

The first people of Canada are comprised of many tribes, Indian and Inuit, but all of them have in common a deep spiritual relationship with the land and nature. They see themselves as being part of a world of interrelated spiritual forms. They revere the animals, the trees, and the land. In past times, those who hunted for their food treated the animals they hunted with great respect. A hunter would talk or sing to the bear before killing it, assuring the animal that its death was necessary only because the hunter and his family needed food. A tree would not be cut down for a canoe until its spirit was first appeased.

Myths were very important. They told of the story of creation, the origin of the moon, the sun, and the stars, and explained the meanings of various religious rituals. Visions and dreams had great significance. Young Hurons would seek a vision of their guardian spirit, who would reveal to them their personal chant that they were to sing when in danger. Many tribes had an elite group of shamans (medicine men) who had great powers and could

Opposite: **Easter Mass inside Quebec's Catholic Notre Dame Cathedral.**

Below: **Inuit funeral mask. The Inuit believe that specters and ghosts haunt the world.**

Statues of Canada's original church fathers keep watch over Quebec City.

heal the sick. Ojibway Indians underwent a purification ritual, entering a sweat lodge where the scented vapors of an intensely hot, herbal sauna cleansed their bodies and spirits.

Both the Hurons and Iroquois had curing societies. The Iroquois False Face Curing Society used carved wooden masks they believed possessed a spiritual force that gave special curative powers to those who wore them. The Pacific Coast tribes used masks based on their belief that the human and animal worlds were interconnected. Transformation masks used during religious ceremonies illustrated this link. The masks opened and closed to reveal either a human or animal face as the wearer pulled the strings.

CONVERTING THE NATIVES

Unfortunately, when both the French and the English reached the shores of North America, they saw the natives who lived there as savages and heathens and their task as that of bringing enlightenment to these people. When Jacques Cartier landed on the Gaspé Peninsula and planted his great cross in 1534, he brought with him the beginnings of Christianity to

THE POTLATCH CEREMONY

The potlatch ceremony was a common practice of the Pacific Coast tribes in which a tribal chief invited people to a celebration of feasting, dancing, and gift-giving. Potlatches were held to mark rites of initiation, to mourn the dead, or to celebrate the investiture of a new chief.

At the potlatch, which could last for days, the host chief would present gifts to his guests. The value of the gift would correspond to the guest's social ranking. The greater the prestige of the chief, the more wealth he distributed in gifts. When his guests held their own potlatches, they were expected to give even more lavishly or they would be shamed. A chief who made himself poor by giving lavishly at a potlatch ceremony could count on getting his wealth returned at subsequent potlatch ceremonies where he would be a guest.

The potlatch ceremony was therefore important in establishing the status, rank, and privileges of the Indians. However, it was not understood as being an important ritual by the white, federal government and was banned. This ban was removed in 1951 and potlatches are being held again today, but never on the same scale as the past.

Canada. When Samuel de Champlain followed, he brought with him four grey-robed Recollet friars of the Franciscan order. They were the first missionaries from France, and they were quickly followed by Jesuits, Sulpicians, Ursulines, and others.

While the adventurers and explorers strove to monopolize the fur trade and the land, the missionaries spread their faith. Not surprisingly, the missionaries were often frustrated and met with disaster in their attempts to convert the Indians. Many of them gave their lives for their cause, such as the Jesuit priest Jean de Brébeuf and his fellow missionary, Gabriel Lalemant, who suffered a horrifying death at the hands of the Iroquois in 1649.

FIRST NORTH AMERICAN SAINT The first North American Indian saint was Kateri Tekakwitha, known as the Lily of the Mohawks. Determined to live a life of virginity, she rejected several offers of marriage. This put her at odds with Mohawk Indian society even before she was baptized a Christian in 1676. She was persecuted and left home for the St. Francois-Xavier Mission in Quebec. There, she made a private vow of chastity and became known for her sanctity. She died in 1680 and was beatified in 1980.

French explorer Jacques Cartier said: "... (finding the natives) living without God and without religion like brute beasts, I thereupon concluded in my private judgment that I should be committing a great sin if I did not make it my business to devise some means of bringing them to the knowledge of God."

CLAIMING THEIR OWN

As settlers began to open up the continent, the church was their constant companion and source of comfort in an undiscovered, hostile land. The English colonies were predominantly Protestant while New France was Roman Catholic.

The French clergy, who faced so much opposition in their attempts to convert the Indians, had a much easier time among their own people. They set up schools and hospitals, collected church tithes from the farmers, and had a powerful, moral influence in French-Canadian society. Marie Guyart, an Ursuline nun, came to Canada in 1639 and opened a convent and school. She ministered to both the leaders of New France and little Indian girls and earned for herself the title of "spiritual mother of New France."

There were Anglican military and naval chaplains in Newfoundland and Nova Scotia before 1750, but the thrust of Anglicanism in Canada came with the flood of Protestant Loyalist refugees who fled north during the American Revolution.

THE PIONEER CHURCH

Though seldom architecturally imposing, what the pioneer churches lacked in splendor they made up for in devotion. In the early days, there was seldom stone or the ingredients for brick-making, but timber was abundant, so the pioneer church was often built of wood. Many churches were made of logs. (It was the Swedes and Germans who introduced log cabin construction into Canada.) The building of a church was a community event in which everyone would lend a hand. While the men worked to fell the trees, haul the logs, and put up the building, the women cooked to feed them all. When completed, the church became the hub of the settlers' lives. Sunday was a time when men could relax, women could socialize, children could play, and everyone would be dressed in their finest.

ROOM FOR ALL BELIEFS

Others that came after the English and the French also brought with them their own churches. The Dutch arrived with their Dutch Reformed Church, Lutherans came from Sweden and Germany. The Scots introduced Presbyterianism when they emigrated to Nova Scotia in the 19th century. Immigrants from Asia brought their beliefs—Buddhism, Sikhism, Hinduism, and Islam. The empty lands of the prairies offered a refuge for a number of oppressed minority groups, among them the Mennonites, Ukrainians, Doukhobors, and Jews who left Russia for Canada. Today, there are many such small religious groups who have resisted all pressures to change.

RELIGION AND MULTICULTURALISM

The Canadian emphasis on multiculturalism has also had its effect on religion. Canadians feel people have a right to express their views, but these views should not be forced on anyone. Canadians appear to be tolerant of religious differences and not overly enthusiastic about evangelism. Christian and non-Christian alike are free to practice their own forms of religion. Thus, while Christian churches of all denominations are a standard feature in all towns and cities in Canada, wherever there are groups of people of other religious affiliations, they are free to build and worship in their own temple, mosque, or synagogue.

Saskatchewan Cree Chief Thunderchild in the late 19th century said: "The white men have offered us two forms of religion: the Roman Catholic and the Protestant. But we in our Indian bands have our own religion. Why is that not accepted too? It is the worship of one God, and it was the strength of our people for centuries."

LANGUAGE

SOMEONE ONCE SAID, the difference between the United States and Canada is that Canadians speak French! This is a rather inaccurate way of putting things, as not all Canadians speak French, but it is true that in Canada, there are two official languages—English and French—while in the United States, everybody has to learn English.

Sociologists and statisticians divide the Canadian population into a spectrum of francophones, anglophones, and allophones. A francophone is a person whose mother tongue is French. An anglophone is someone whose mother tongue is English, and an allophone is someone whose mother tongue is neither English nor French.

DIVIDED BY TONGUES

The main languages spoken in Canada are English and French because these are the languages of the original colonizers of the land. Today, the English-speaking community is distributed fairly evenly across Canada, but French-speaking Canadians are concentrated in the provinces of Quebec, New Brunswick, Ontario, and parts of Manitoba.

English is the mother tongue for most Canadians, except in Quebec, where many speak French, and the Northwest Territories, where many natives speak their own language. The proportion of Canadians who cite English as their mother tongue has been on the increase since 1941 in all provinces except Quebec and Ontario. In Ontario, because of the immigrants who are attracted to this area, the number of allophones has increased sharply since 1941. In 1986, Ontario had the largest allophone population in Canada, making up almost half of all the allophones in the country.

Opposite: **In Kitchener, Ontario, there are newspapers printed in German for the town's German-speaking community.**

Below: **A sign in Ottawa illustrates Canada's widespread bilingualism.**

Other main languages that can be heard, apart from French and English, are Dutch in Prince Edward Island, Greek in Quebec, German in Ontario, German and Ukrainian in the prairie provinces of Manitoba, Saskatchewan, and Alberta, and Chinese in British Columbia. Since the 1960s, the use of Asian languages, especially Chinese, Vietnamese, Punjabi, Hindi, and Urdu, has grown considerably.

Native and English bilingual sign at a Hudson's Bay Company station in the Northwest Territories.

CANADIAN ENGLISH

English is the most widely spoken language in the world. But depending on where one is in the world, the English that is spoken can be very different. Following this trend, therefore, Canadians speak their very own brand of English.

Think of Canadian English as a dialect that is the result of both British and American influences as well as being distinctively Canadian too. Generations of immigrants who came from Britain are responsible for those British accents that are discernable in Canadian speech, while Americans have also had great influence. Most of the differences that Americans notice in Canadian speech are due to the influence of the English, while English visitors notice that there are many features that are common to both American and Canadian English.

This is true of the spoken as well as the written language. For example, where Canadians would say blinds, taps, serviettes, and chesterfield, Americans would say shades, faucets, napkins, and sofa. Then again, Canadians would say fall, depot, creek, and fries, while the English would say autumn, station, stream, and chips. Canadians pronounce tomato, dance, half, and clerk like Americans do, but pronounce been, lever, ration, and the letter Z like the English. Canadians and Americans don't always spell the same way either, because Canadians have kept some English styles of writing, for example: color is "colour," center is "centre," and ax is "axe." However, the almost uninterrupted flow of books, magazines, television, radio, and movies from south of the border and the movement and interaction of people both ways is such that American English is gaining greater influence, especially among young Canadians.

This sign in a Toronto train station illustrates how English and French can be seen alongside each other on all public notices.

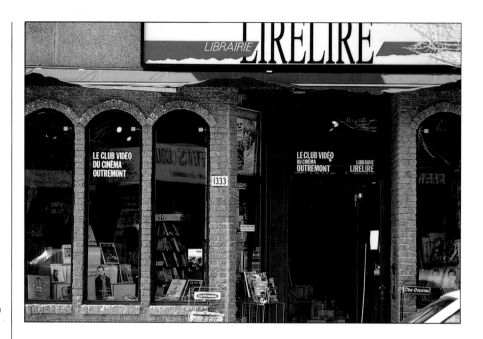

L'libraire—a French bookshop in Quebec.

CANADIAN FRENCH

French, as it is spoken in Canada, is not a *patois* (dialect) or a pidgin mixture of French, English, and Indian language. It is authentic French, brought to the country by the fewer than 10,000 original colonists who settled in New France in the 17th century. At that time, the French who came spoke the various dialects of their birthplaces, but by the time the British took over the country with the Treaty of Paris in 1763, a Canadian French had developed and had become the common language of the immigrants.

Cut off from France, French Canadians continued to develop a distinctly different language from that spoken in Europe. Increasingly under siege by the growing number of English-speaking newcomers, they resisted outside influence and developed a fierce pride that made them cling to their culture and language.

Today, French universities in Quebec do considerable research into the language and l'Académie Canadienne-Française, l'Office de la Langue Française, and le Ministère d'Affaires Culturelles are entrusted with the task of seeing that Canadian French continues to flourish in the country.

NATIVE LANGUAGES

Naturally, before either the French or English arrived in Canada, the native people had fully functioning societies with their own languages. But they did not all speak one language. Anthropologists and linguists have classified the languages spoken by the natives of Canada into 11 language families—Algonkian, Iroquoian, Siouan, Athapaskan, Kootenayan, Salishan, Wakashan, Tsimshian, Haida, Tlingit, and Eskimo-Aleut. Together, these 11 families are comprised of 53 individual languages.

Natives who belong to the same language family do not necessarily share the same culture. The Blackfoot of the plains and the Micmac of the Maritimes, for example, belong to the Algonkian family, but their cultures are very different.

Of the native languages that are still spoken in Canada, only three seem to be surviving—Cree (Algonkian), Ojibwa (Algonkian), and Inuktitut (Eskimo-Aleut). The others are in decline, although there is an increasing interest among the natives themselves in trying to preserve what remains by teaching their language to the younger generation.

Even missing persons reports appear in two languages.

ARTS

IN THE PAST, Canadians thought of themselves as a people with no culture or tradition that could be identified as "Canadian." They had their English and French traditions that were later supplemented by the cultures of other immigrant European minorities. Many also felt that there was little to distinguish the artistic endeavors of Canadians. To find recognition, writers and·artists had to go south of the border. But times have changed, and few today would doubt that there is a distinctly Canadian tradition in the books, art, drama, movies, and music that are now being produced. But much debate still rages as to the true identity of Canadian art.

NATIVE ART

Before the arrival of the Europeans, the native cultures of the Indian and Inuit peoples already existed. These cultures were stimulated by the coming of the Europeans, when the introduction of metal tools enabled the natives, especially the West Coast Indians and the Inuit, to create abundant and more daring artifacts. Art was very much a part of the daily lives of the people. Song, dance, and mime were essential elements of native cultures used to summon the spirits, ask for guidance, and predict the future. Images carved out of bone, stone, and wood were considered to have magical qualities and served to tell stories of their ancestors to the young. Pottery, basketry, and weaving produced items for daily use. Drums were used in religious ceremonies. It was only when these objects were "discovered" by the new Canadians that native artists began to produce works that had a commercial value. A few artists have managed to go beyond this commercialization. Two well-known native artists who have high reputations are Bill Reid, known for his incredible carvings, and Robert Davidson, whose totem poles can be found in New York, Japan, and Switzerland.

Opposite: **Some interesting "street art" in Montreal, Quebec.**

Below: **Indian house totem pole from the Northwest Territories. The eagle at the top represents the Thunder Bird, which was believed to bring rain to prevent the crops from drying up.**

An exhibition hall of Canada's National Gallery in Ottawa. The gallery contains the most distinguished collection of Canadian and European paintings in the country.

CANADIAN ART

Early Canadian paintings were often romanticized depictions of Canadian landscape and life. Thomas Davies presented the viewer with pleasing and vivid but unreal watercolors of the Canadian landscape, while the canvases of Paul Kane, who traveled from east to west to study and record the Indian cultures, portrayed Indian life in an idealized and heroic manner.

It was Quebec painter' Ozias Leduc and James Wilson Morrice of Montreal who began to paint a distinctive Canadian landscape and lifestyle as they actually saw it. After their experiments came the works of Canada's most famous school of artists, the Group of Seven—Lawren Harris, A.Y. Jackson, Arthur Lismer, Frederick Varley, Franklin Carmichael, Franz Johnston, and J.E.H. MacDonald. These seven artists were inspired by the works of fellow Canadian Tom Thomson, an artist and outdoorsman. Nature was their theme, and they recorded the forms and colors of the northern Ontario landscape as it had never been done before—brutal, rugged landscapes, rocks fractured and cracked by frost, trees blasted by fierce storms, villages clinging to gullied slopes.

They were followed in the 1930s by a group of French-Canadian painters—Alfred Pellan, Paul-Emile Borduas, Jacques de Tonnancour, and Jean-Paul Riopelle—who painted in the modernist experimental manner that was the trend in the art centers of Paris and New York.

Paintings by David Milne and Emily Carr are also considered Canadian classics. Carr, a West Coast artist, depicted the great forests of giant cedar and fir and was greatly influenced by the art of the West Coast Indians. She became the first woman artist to achieve fame in Canadian art. Later

Canadian artists of note are Jack Shadbolt, another painter from western Canada who was similarly influenced by West Coast Indian images, and Robert Bateman, painter and celebrator of Canadian wildlife.

There is no single center of art in Canada, but artists work and exhibit all across the country from Newfoundland to Vancouver Island.

CANADIAN WRITERS

The first Canadian writers used a descriptive style and told stories of Canadian life. Susanna Moodie and Catharine Parr Traill, for instance, were two English sisters who came from a comfortable life in England and had to adapt to the harsh realities of life in the Canadian bush. Moodie's *Roughing it in the Bush* and *Life in the Clearings* and Traill's *The Backwoods of Canada* describe the hardships of their pioneer existence. Satire found expression in the works of Stephen Leacock, whose *Sunshine Sketches of a Little Town* was an ironic, humorous look at small-town Ontario provincial life; Thomas Chandler Haliburton's *The Clockmaker; or, the Sayings and Doings of Sam Slick of Slickville*, and Thomas McCulloch's *Letters of Mephibosheth Stepsure* are other humorous pieces.

The fame of *Anne of Green Gables*, a fictional story of a lovable Canadian girl by Prince Edward Island author Lucy Maud Montgomery, has certainly spread beyond the borders of this large country. Other modern Canadian writers to have achieved international fame include Ethel Wilson, Hugh MacLennan, Margaret Laurence, Mordecai Richler, Margaret Atwood, Alice Munroe, Robertson Davies, Morley Callaghan, and Leonard Cohen.

Who's this famous lady? As in many countries, caricaturists sell their skills and wares in the street. This one is of Queen Elizabeth II.

Native storytelling is largely oral. A hostile policy toward Indians encouraged the native people to be assimilated into the white population rather than celebrate their distinctiveness. But the 1970s proved a turning point when an enormous range of native creative writing began to appear and then to flower in the 1980s. Some Indian writers of note are Maria Campbell, Basil Johnston, Rita Joe, Daniel David Moses, Beatrice Culleton, Jeannette Armstrong, Ruby Slipperjack, and Thomson Highway.

CANADA IN VERSE In poetry, Confederation was received with enthusiasm by the Confederation Poets of the 1890s, such as Bliss Carman, Charles Roberts, Archibald Lampman, and Duncan Campbell Scott. Roberts and Lampman wrote of rural life in the maritime provinces and Ontario. Scott observed the Indians of the north.

Michael Ondaatje, Booker prize winner of 1992.

TEN BOOKS TO READ

There is much to be learned about Canada—whether about life on the prairies or the French-English dichotomy—from the books of these Canadian writers:

- Lucy Maud Montgomery: *Anne of Green Gables* (1908), the adventures of a young and lovable Canadian girl.
- Morley Callaghan: *Such is My Beloved* (1934), a moving account of conflict between spiritual love and the realities of city living.
- Hugh MacLennan: *Two Solitudes* (1945), on the relationship between French and English Canadians.
- W.O. Mitchell: *Who Has Seen the Wind?* (1947), a picture of life on the prairies.
- Gabrielle Roy: *The Tin Flute* (1947), the conflict that results when the old French order and values clash with Anglo-American materialism.
- Mordecai Richler: *The Apprenticeship of Duddy Kravitz* (1959), the story of a young Jew from Montreal.
- Farley Mowat: *Never Cry Wolf* (1963), a tale of the north.
- Anne Hébert: *Kamouraska* (1970), based on a true story of a love-triangle murder that took place in Canada in 1840.
- Margaret Laurence: *The Stone Angel* (1964), a powerfully told story of an elderly woman who struggles with the indignities of old age.
- Margaret Atwood: *The Handmaid's Tale* (1985), a frightening view of the future.

In the 1930s, Canadian poetry expressed Canadian ideals and aspirations in the works of E.J. Pratt, A.J.M. Smith, F.R. Scott, and A.M. Klein. Pratt wrote epics on historic themes (Brébeuf, the Jesuit missionary; the building of the Canadian Pacific). Smith's best-known poem on Canada is *The Lonely Land*, in which he celebrates the rugged, rocky, and wind-torn Canadian Shield. Scott and Klein expressed a broad humanistic and cosmopolitan view of Canada in the world.

Among modern Canadian poets are Michael Ondaatje, Phyllis Webb, Margaret Atwood, Leonard Cohen, and Alden Nowlan. Michael Ondaatje in particular has recently risen to fame by winning the British Booker prize (1992) for his novel, *The English Patient*.

An intermission at a local playhouse in the Yukon Territory.

PERFORMING ARTS

Mary Pickford, Lorne Greene, Christopher Plummer, Raymond Massey, William Shatner—these are all Canadians who made their careers in London, New York, and Hollywood. Many more followed their path, because for many years it was necessary for talented Canadians to go south of the border to find due recognition. Happily, this is changing as Canadians are becoming more aware and appreciative of home-grown talent.

Most Canadian cities have small theaters that present the works of Canadian playwrights. The Canada Council gives grants to theaters, opera and dance companies, orchestras, and arts councils in the various municipalities to help promote and support their activities. In the 1970s, hundreds of new Canadian plays were written after the Canada Council insisted that at least half of the productions held in Canadian theaters had to have Canadian content.

The Canadian music industry grew from a base of folk songs, dance tunes, and religious and patriotic music. Canadian singers and song writers were major factors in the popularity of folk music in the 1960s, while the 1970s and 1980s saw the rise of many Canadian rock groups.

Many big cities like Vancouver and Toronto have symphony orchestras. There are three major dance companies in the country—the Royal Winnipeg Ballet, the National Ballet of Canada, and Les Grands Ballets Canadiens. The annual Shakespeare Festival at Stratford, Ontario, and the annual Shaw Festival at Niagara-on-the-Lake, Ontario, are international events. In smaller towns and cities, there is no lack of artistic activity even though it may be on a much smaller scale. Arts-active people get together to form their own choral, symphonic, and theatrical groups.

THE SHAKESPEARE FESTIVAL

The Shakespeare Festival at Stratford, Ontario has gained for itself an international reputation for its presentation of Shakespeare's plays. It is considered to be one of the three great Shakespearean theaters of the English-speaking world, the other two being the National Theater in London, England, and Britain's Royal Shakespeare Company. It was started by the Irish director Tyrone Guthrie in 1953. Today, the festival is celebrated in three theaters—the Third Stage, which is used for workshops, experimental plays, and actor training; the 1,100-seat Avon Theater; and the main 2,200-seat Festival Theater, which is a modern version of the traditional Elizabethan theater. Millions of people come to Stratford to enjoy classical and modern plays and music productions during the festival, which usually runs from May to October.

IN THE NEWS

Canada is so large that it has been very difficult to distribute a national newspaper or magazine. Every town has its own local newspaper, usually a weekly publication, dealing with events of interest to the community. Larger daily newspapers, like the *Vancouver Sun*, the *Toronto Star*, and the *Montreal Gazette*, unite the communities of each province by providing news of regional, national, and international interest. There is no national newspaper, though the *Globe and Mail* is probably the closest thing to it—it is published in Toronto, but is distributed in all the provinces.

Canada has its own English language news magazine, called *Maclean's*. *L'Actualité* is the French language equivalent. American news magazines such as *Newsweek* and a Canadian edition of *Time* are read by many Canadians. There is also a wide range of Canadian-published magazines that deal with all sorts of interests, from art to computers. The *Canadian Forum* deals with political issues and is an ardent supporter of Canadian arts, *Chatelaine* is a leading women's magazine, and *Saturday Night* has something for every member of the family.

Examples of American publications on sale in Canada.

95

A NATIONAL IMAGE

CBC and NFB—these initials stand for the Canadian Broadcasting Corporation and the National Film Board—are two organizations that have done much to create a national image for the media.

The CBC is Canada's national radio and television service. It began as a Crown corporation, or government company, in 1936, inspired partly by the example of the British Broadcasting Corporation. It was also an attempt to answer the threat of American programming to Canadian cultural sovereignty. From the original eight broadcasting stations, it grew to the hundreds that are now operating all over the country. It provides regular newscasts, with news of national and international importance, as well as light and educational entertainment. The NFB was founded just before

The Canada Council was created in 1957. Its function is to encourage the development of the arts. In order to do this, it has a large fund from which it gives grants to individual artists, organizations, and professional associations to help them in their cultural activities.

Right: **People line up to see some of the many American movies shown in Canada.**

Opposite: **Raymond Massey, one of Canada's most illustrious stage and screen actors.**

World War II by John Grierson, a Scotsman who was entrusted with the task of creating a film company whose films would "interpret Canada to Canadians." The NFB has made many award-winning films and documentaries, teaching Canadians about their country and people.

THE GENIE AWARDS

The first Canadian Film Awards were presented in 1949 in Ottawa. They were awarded to promote Canadian artists and to raise movie standards. The last awards were given in 1978; in 1979, the Academy of Canadian Cinema was formed to continue this work. The academy now presents a Genie award to the best Canadian feature movie of the year. Recent winners have been *My American Cousin* (1986), *The Decline of the American Empire* (1987), *Un Zoo La Nuit* (1988), *Dead Ringers* (1989), and *Jesus de Montreal* (1990).

CANADIAN CONTENT

The media is the area in which American influence is most pervasive. American magazines, books, and movies are found in bookstores and libraries everywhere. In view of this, the federal government set up the Canadian Radio-Television and Telecommunications Commission to control the Canadian communications industry. The CRTC lays down rules to ensure that the programming of Canadian radio stations and television channels contains a substantial percentage of programs that are of Canadian origin. As a result, there is now a high proportion of Canadian content on radio and television, and much of it is of very good quality.

LEISURE

THE AVERAGE CANADIAN today works a five-day 35–40 hour week. He or she looks forward to at least two weeks' paid vacation and nine public holidays a year. With all these holidays, it has been estimated that the average Canadian enjoys a minimum of 124 leisure days a year, and many Canadians actually enjoy more. This leisure time is spent in many ways.

SPORTS

There is no doubt that Canadians are a great sporting people. No matter what the weather may be, from 80°F in summer to 20°F in winter, there is a sport that will fit the bill. Many Canadian sporting activities, such as tobogganing, snowshoeing, lacrosse, and canoeing, owe their existence to the native Indians. But the games that are most important to Canadians are hockey, football, and baseball. Canadians share a love for all these games with Americans. Such sports are also a means for Canadians to display their national pride, cheering their teams on the playing field in international competitions.

HOCKEY Hockey, when mentioned in the Canadian context, almost always means ice hockey and not field hockey, which is played on grass. Ice hockey is as Canadian a game as can be. It is a Canadian invention, the brainchild of a group of soldiers in Kingston, Ontario, who tied blades to their boots and used field hockey sticks and an old lacrosse ball to relieve the monotony of garrison duty one winter day in 1855. Today, it is the game that binds all. Watching a hockey game, either on television on Saturday nights or in the local arena where it is played, is almost a ritual. The television program, "Hockey Night in Canada," is the longest-running TV show in the country—the first program was aired in 1952, which means it has been running for more than 40 years!

Opposite: **Skiing is a very popular sport in Canada. This man is taking part in the 1988 Olympic slalom held in Calgary, Alberta.**

Ice hockey is a very physical game and is played with much passion in Canada.

Canadians learn to love the sport from a very early age. The moment school is out, bags are tossed aside and goal posts set up in the neighborhood cul de sac, where half a dozen kids or so clash with hockey sticks to put an old tennis ball into the net. In winter, the scene is played on frozen ponds and streams.

The childhood of a Canadian boy often includes dreams of becoming a big hockey star in the National Hockey League (NHL). Parents give up hours of their time taking these aspiring NHL players to and from games and practices.

Canadian teams such as the Montreal Canadiens, the Edmonton Oilers, the Quebec Nordiques, the Toronto Maple Leafs and the Vancouver Canucks, as well as American teams like the Chicago Blackhawks and Detroit Red Wings, are members of the NHL. In Hockey's Hall of Fame are Canadian players such as Bobby Orr, Bobby Hull, and "Rocket" Maurice Richard. The current hockey superstar is Wayne Gretzky, who plays for the Los Angeles Kings. Gretzky won the Hart Trophy for the most valuable player eight times in a row, from 1980 to 1987.

HOCKEY, THE RELIGION OF CONVENIENCE

Relating how hockey and the church helped to keep prairie communities together, Ken Dryden, author and former goal tender for the Montreal Canadiens, said in a television series on the game: "Hockey came later, the religion of convenience, linking communities together, town to town, region to region. For young and old, something to talk about, to share, a distraction from the long idle winters, a way to create and strengthen the community's bonds."

BASEBALL Baseball is an American game that has captured a large Canadian following. Baseball diamonds are a necessary feature of Canadian towns and cities everywhere. The game has been played in Canada as a professional game for over a century. However, only two Canadian professional teams—the Toronto Blue Jays and the Montreal Expos—compete with American teams in the World Series. In 1992, for the first time since the World Series began, a Canadian team—the Toronto Blue Jays—won the trophy. It was celebrated as a great Canadian victory even though the Blue Jays' players had come from everywhere—the United States, South America, and the Caribbean islands. The Toronto Sky Dome is the home of Canadian baseball. It was built at a cost of over $400 million and has a retractable roof that can cover the stadium when the weather is bad.

Crowds fill the stadium in Toronto to watch a baseball game.

CANADIAN FOOTBALL The game of football, another Canadian invention, was derived from the British game of rugby. It was brought to Canada by immigrants and introduced to the United States by players from McGill University who were in Cambridge, Massachusetts, to play football with a team from Harvard. When they arrived in Cambridge, the McGill players found that Harvard played a version of soccer. To solve the problem, the teams played two games, each under the other's rules. The Harvard team liked the Canadian version so much that they introduced it to other American teams. American football players soon introduced their own rules, thus creating American football.

Canadian football has slightly different rules, and the game is played on a larger field and with 12 players a side instead of 11 as in the United

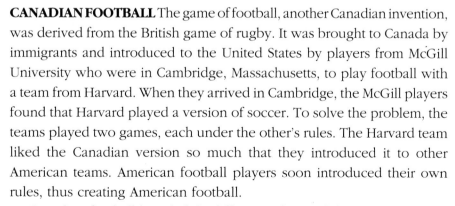

Canoeing is a highly popular outdoor activity in Canada. These canoeists are setting out on the Yukon River in the Yukon Territory.

States. Huge football stadiums with floodlights are a familiar landmark in Canadian cities. Football is played in high schools and colleges, but is most popular in the big universities. The Canadian Football League is the equivalent of the National Football League in the United States. All the major cities have their own professional football teams, such as the Calgary Stampeders, the Ottawa Rough Riders, the Edmonton Eskimos, the Winnipeg Blue Bombers, and the BC Lions. Many of the players are, however, Americans.

LACROSSE This is the oldest Canadian game still being played today. It was founded on an Indian game called *baggataway*, which was played as a means to develop group discipline and personal ingenuity. When the French came, the game appealed to them so much that they developed it into lacrosse, a truly Canadian sport. The first lacrosse club was formed in Montreal in 1839. In 1867, the game became so popular that the National Lacrosse Association of Canada was formed, the first national sports organization in the country.

THE LURE OF THE WILD

For many Canadians, the wilderness is literally just outside the door. Those who live in the rural areas, or even in the suburbs of big cities, have access to parks and forests that are little more than minutes away. Perhaps it is this proximity to nature that has made Canadians such an outdoor-loving people.

Canadians engage in a wide variety of outdoor activities that reflect Canada's physical geography. In summer, city dwellers migrate whenever possible to cottages, parks, and resorts scattered across the vast network of lakes and rivers for which Canada is justly famous. Canoeing, boating, hiking, and camping are popular from coast to coast.

Hunting and fishing are also popular activities all year round, but a licence has to be obtained first. Hunters shoot many types of game, from small birds like grouse and ducks to big animals like deer, moose, and bear. But there are special seasons for certain kinds of game and a limit to the number that a hunter can shoot. Sport fishing can be enjoyed on inland lakes and rivers as well as in the ocean. Ice fishing is also a popular winter pastime. Trout, salmon, and pike are just a few of the many types of fish available.

Skiing, either downhill or cross-country, is almost the natural thing to do in a country where winters are comparatively long and almost certainly accompanied by snow. Skiing is possible almost anywhere in Canada where there are high hills and mountains, and Canadian downhill ski resorts, such as those in the Western Cordillera of British Columbia and Alberta, and the Laurentian Highlands of Quebec, north of Montreal and Quebec City, are world famous.

Skidooing or snowmobiling is a mechanical form of skiing. The skidoo or snowmobile is a Canadian invention. It is like a motorcycle and tractor combined with two skis in front and tracks behind. It provides the rider with the exhilaration and speed of motorcycling and the joys of playing in a winter wonderland.

NATIONAL AND PROVINCIAL PARKS

In order that Canadians may always enjoy the outdoors, there are many national and provincial parks, areas of wilderness that have been preserved for the enjoyment of all. Canada got its first national park as early as 1885, when hot springs were discovered at Banff during the construction of the Canadian Pacific Railway. The Banff National Park in the Rocky Mountains was the first in an extensive national and provincial park system. This now includes more than 50,000 square miles of reserved land including such diverse regions as the Pacific Rim National Park on the Pacific coast, the Point Pelee Bird Sanctuary in Ontario, and the Fundy National Park on the Atlantic coast—all managed by the federal government.

Many other smaller provincial parks, managed by the various provincial governments, dot the country. Facilities available in these parks vary. There are no roads in wilderness areas. Campers must leave their vehicles at the entrance to the parks and hike many miles inland, carrying all

Fishing at one of Canada's many national parks—a great way to relax.

LEARNING TO HUNT

Many schools and colleges teach a special course on outdoor recreation that prepares students who want to go hunting. In British Columbia, for instance, the course is called Conservation and Outdoor Recreation. Anyone over the age of 14 who wishes to buy a gun and get a hunting licence must complete this course. It teaches students essential outdoor skills such as safety and survival techniques, how to handle firearms, and how to identity animals and birds. Hunting laws, regulations, and ethics are also taught.

their camping gear on their backs. In other parks, it is possible to drive right up to the camp site, which may accommodate either tents or large recreational vehicles. Some parks even have flush toilets and hot showers.

HOME ENTERTAINMENT

There are many Canadians who spend much of their leisure at home with hobbies such as cultivating the arts, at craft work, or tending the garden.

It is the dream of most Canadians to own their own home, and when they do, much of their leisure time is spent on ways to improve their home. There is a handy workshop hidden in many garages and basements, filled with all kinds of mechanical and electrical tools. The garden is another favorite preoccupation. Canadians look forward to the first frost-free day so they can begin working outside, planting flowers or seeding a small vegetable garden.

Much leisure time is also spent passively. Canadians love watching television—there is a television set in almost every home. And the number of homes with video tape recorders, compact disk players, and home computers is ever increasing.

TRAVEL

Canadians love to travel and collectively spend a lot more money overseas than tourists who come to Canada. The United States is the most popular destination, accounting for more than 90% of all trips abroad. Canadians love the United States because it is warmer there, has many attractions, and the goods are generally cheaper than at home. Other favorite destinations are Europe (especially the United Kingdom, France and Germany), the Caribbean, Mexico, Hong Kong, and Japan.

An unusual mixture of indoor and outdoor entertainment—enjoying the fresh air while watching television! Canadians spend an average of 23 hours a week in front of the television.

FESTIVALS

ON ANY DAY, somewhere in Canada, a festival or special event of some kind is bound to be taking place. It may be a celebration that Canadians share with many other people in the world, like Christmas, or it may be a grand Canadian event of international fame, like Stratford's Shakespeare Festival or the Calgary Stampede. Or it could also be a small community celebrating some special attraction in its area or some bit of local history.

CHRISTMAS AND EASTER

Christmas and Easter are two festivals that are of great importance to Christians in Canada. Everyone knows that December 25th is traditionally celebrated as the birthday of Jesus Christ, the central focus of Christianity. But Jesus Christ has a difficult time vying with Santa Claus for center stage. Christmas is celebrated as much in the shopping malls as in the churches. Long before December comes, advertisements in the newspapers and on the radio and television remind people that they have to begin shopping for gifts.

Family and friends gather for a Christmas dinner, most traditionally consisting of turkey, ham, and, less commonly, goose as well as mince pies and Christmas pudding. A Christmas tree trimmed with lights and decorations and an angel or a star on top, and the presents below it, are all indispensable elements of the festivities. Many people love to decorate their houses with outdoor lights to add color to this holiday season. For Christians, going to church on Christmas Eve and Christmas Day is an important element of the celebration.

Easter is observed usually in late March or April and has retained more of its religious flavor. Christians prepare for Easter with a more sober

Opposite: **The Royal Canadian Mounted Police on parade on July 1, Canada Day.**

Below: **Ottawa's Caribbean people celebrate their heritage.**

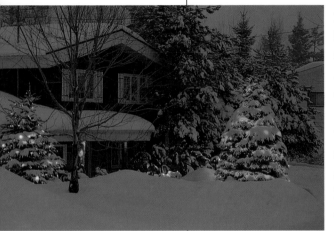

Canada's snowy winters are ideal for creating a classic white Christmas.

period of 40 days called Lent. The end of Lent is marked by Good Friday, when the suffering and death of Jesus Christ on the cross is remembered. All this sorrow is banished on Easter Sunday, when Christians believe that Christ rose from the dead.

Hot cross buns are associated with this time of the year. These are small loaves of bread, spiced and sweetened and marked with a cross on the surface. Easter bunnies and colorful chocolate Easter eggs are also a part of the season—the custom comes from a tradition, older than Christianity, that believed the rabbit to be a symbol of fertility and eggs to be symbolic of new life.

THANKSGIVING

In a country that used to have an agricultural economy, harvest time has always been a time for thanksgiving. Despite the fact that people are becoming more removed from the land today, this tradition of giving thanks for a good harvest has continued. In Canada, the celebration of Thanksgiving falls on the second Monday of October. In America, however, Thanksgiving is celebrated on the fourth Thursday of November and is a festival closely connected to the history of the Pilgrim Fathers.

Except for the fact that it is on a different day and celebrated for different reasons, the actual celebration of Thanksgiving is much the same no matter which side of the border one is on. Family members do their best to come home to be with each other and to enjoy a Thanksgiving dinner of roast turkey with cranberry sauce and all the trimmings.

HALLOWEEN

This is one festival that is exclusively for children. Halloween is the eve of All Saints Day. All Saints Day falls on October 31, but is not a public holiday. On the night of October 31, young children look forward to dressing up in all kinds of costumes and going from house to house yelling "trick or treat." Adults buy lots of candies and sweets to hand to the children. The younger children are often accompanied by their parents or older brothers and sisters.

Fireworks are not usually displayed on Halloween, but are commonly used either on Victoria Day or Canada Day.

REMEMBRANCE DAY

No matter how many years may pass, Canadians will always remember those who died while fighting for freedom in the two world wars and the Korean War. Remembrance Day, known as Veterans Day in the United States, is celebrated on November 11, because the armistice that officially ended World War I happened at the 11th hour of the 11th day of the 11th month, that is, 11 a.m. on November 11, 1918.

In Canadian towns and cities, members of the Royal Canadian Legion, together with other uniformed groups and service clubs, gather to pay their respects to the dead. The Remembrance Day ceremony usually includes a recitation of "In Flanders Fields," a poem by the late Colonel John McCrae, a native of Guelph, Ontario.

Pumpkin heads on spooky scarecrow figures greet trick-or-treaters on Halloween. Hollowed out and carved with a grinning face, pumpkins also make glowing jack o' lanterns on Halloween.

CANADA DAY

Canada Day, or Dominion Day as it used to be called, is celebrated on July 1. It is the anniversary of the creation of the Dominion of Canada in 1867. Towns and cities all over the country hold their own small ceremonies on this day to celebrate the unity of the country.

Montreal's Scottish community celebrates its origins with a bagpipe procession.

The year 1992 was a special one for Canadians because it was the year they celebrated the 125th birthday of the country. Encouraged by the government and media, "Canada 125" celebrations took place all over the country. People expressed their love for their country in many ways, such as by bicycling from coast to coast, by creating a multi-textured quilt to which many Canadians contributed a square, and by planting trees.

CELEBRATING ORIGINS

Canadians come from all backgrounds, and this multi-cultural nature of Canadian society can be seen in the way people of different origins, religions, and traditions continue to celebrate these differences.

Long before the Europeans came, the native people marked their year with festivals celebrating the seasons or religious rituals. The Ojibway Indians held thanksgiving celebrations in the spring to celebrate the end of winter and in the fall for the bountiful harvest. Indians of the west coast held ceremonial feasts called potlatches, and the plains Indians held *powwows*, or ceremonies of healing. In a more modern way, visitors who go to Brantford, Ontario, in August can take part in the Six Nations Native Pageant, an Iroquois celebration of the tribe's culture and history.

POWWOW

The word *powwow* comes from the old Algonquin word for "medicine man." These days, it is an inter-tribal gathering that celebrates the rituals and spiritual beliefs of the native people. The *powwow* is held over a number of days, during which there is almost nonstop singing, dancing, and drumming, and a continuous parade of traditional and ceremonial native costumes and arts and crafts. Like the healing ceremonies performed by the medicine men of the past, the modern-day *powwow* is a healing and unifying ritual that allows native Indians to display their pride in their culture.

The oldest European immigrants to the country hold festivals during which they display their special foods, crafts, and ways of living. The Festival du Voyageur in St. Boniface, Winnipeg, celebrates the history of the region's early fur traders. The *joie de vivre,* or joy of life, of Quebecers is reflected in le Carnaval de Quebec held in winter. Scottish-Canadians celebrate the annual Highland Games at Antigonish, Nova Scotia, and come together each year for the International Gathering of the Clans, in Pugwash, Nova Scotia.

Ukrainians in the town of Dauphin, Manitoba, hold a National Ukrainian Festival during which the costumes and artifacts of the Ukrainian people are displayed and fiddling contests are held. Vesna Festival, in Saskatoon, Saskatchewan, is another Ukrainian festival of foods and crafts, while Pioneer Days in Steinbach, Manitoba, celebrates the heritage of the Mennonites with a display of threshing, baking, and samples of Mennonite foods. The large Chinese community in Vancouver celebrates the Chinese New Year with dragon dances and firecrackers and all the color and noise that attend it.

At a rodeo competition at the Calgary Stampede, a cowboy tries to see how long he can ride a bucking wild horse—before he is thrown off.

THEME FESTIVALS

Communities all over Canada also create special celebrations that relate to the history of the place or the special attractions of the community. Through these celebrations, community spirit and pride are increased.

Many towns in cattle ranching areas, for instance, have rodeos and fall festivals during which cowboys display their skills and talents. But perhaps the most famous cowboy festival is the Calgary Stampede in July, complete with chuck-wagon races, hot-air balloon races, rodeo showmanship, and agricultural and craft displays.

THE OKANAGAN WINE FESTIVAL

The Okanagan Wine Festival started in 1980 with only a handful of wineries. Today, there are almost 30 and the number is growing. It is a major tourist attraction. As part of the festival, the Calona winery in Kelowna holds a grape-stomp annual championship in which teams of people squash tons of grapes with their feet, cheered on by hundreds of spectators. Wineries uncork their finest products for tasting by a thirsty public.

Many festivals provide a showcase for music, art, drama, crafts, and sports. The town of Banff in the Rocky Mountains has a summer-long Festival of the Arts, which draws thousands of young musicians, singers, dancers, and artists. Edmonton has an annual street performers' festival in July and a Folk Music Festival and Fringe Theater Festival in August.

Climate provides an excellent theme for celebration. The blooming of nature in the spring is the reason for the Annapolis Valley Apple Blossom Festival, Maple Syrup Festival in Plessisville, Quebec, and Tulip Festival in Ottawa. In summer, the pace of festivities picks up with the warmer weather. Food—strawberries, salmon, shrimp, blueberries—is celebrated wherever it is grown or harvested.

HOLIDAYS

Many Canadian public holidays occur either on a Friday or a Monday so that people can enjoy a long weekend. This is important in such a large country where people are very mobile and must travel long distances in order to be with their families.

Almost every Canadian enjoys these national holidays:
- New Year's Day, January 1.
- Good Friday and Easter Monday (dates for both vary according to the Christian calendar).
- Victoria Day, which celebrates Queen Victoria's birthday, the Monday before May 24.
- Canada Day, July 1, celebrated everywhere except in Quebec. In Newfoundland, it is known as Memorial Day and is observed on the Monday nearest July 1.
- Labor Day, the first Monday in September. It is celebrated everywhere except in PEI. It is the last holiday of the summer season, after which it's back to school.
- Thanksgiving, the second Monday in October.
- Christmas Day, December 25.
- Boxing Day, December 26, traditionally a time when Christmas gifts or boxes are given (the Christmas holiday is usually a two-week period for schools that begins with the weekend before Christmas and ends after the New Year).

FOOD

CANADIAN FOOD is difficult to define. In many ways it is very undistinguished. In the fast food restaurants that can be found in small towns and cities alike, one can eat one's fill of hot dogs, hamburgers, and french fries. The menu of a small cafe or restaurant is filled with similar food, plus the standard soups, main courses of meat, potatoes and vegetables, and ice-cream and pie desserts. One university handbook for students describes the basic Canadian meal: "… meat and potatoes plus other vegetables. Eggs, cheese, and fish are common meat substitutes, while spaghetti, noodles, and rice or beans are a few common substitutes for potatoes. Vegetables and fruit are included in most meals. Generally speaking, Canadians do not spice their food heavily."

Fortunately, this is not the complete picture. Canadian food is tremendously varied because it consists of the variety of cuisines that came to Canada with the different peoples who settled here over time.

Opposite: **Some delicious Canadian pears.**

Left: **A Canadian family eats a typical meal of meat, potatoes, and vegetables.**

Codfish being unloaded in New Brunswick.

THE BOUNTY OF THE SEA

As Canada contains nearly a third of all the fresh water in the world in the form of lakes and rivers, fish is abundant all over the country. In the Atlantic provinces of Newfoundland, Prince Edward Island, Nova Scotia, and New Brunswick, fish, especially cod, is available all year round. It can come fresh, dried, pickled, or salted.

In Newfoundland, seal flipper pie is a speciality. To make it you have to scrape away the hair and cut off all the blubber from a seal flipper, then simmer it for a long time and add pork and flour to make a stew-like mixture that is then covered with pastry and made into pies. But the favorite food of Newfoundlanders is probably a boiled dinner of salt pork or beef with potatoes, turnips, carrots, and cabbage.

The food of Nova Scotia reflects the different cuisines of the Scottish, English, German, and French people who settled in the province—fish chowder, Lunenburg sausage with sauerkraut, and Solomon Grundy (a traditional Mennonite recipe of salted herring pickled with vinegar, sugar, and spices).

New Brunswick is known for its clam chowder, made with the large clams from the Shediac region. Dulse is another offering of the sea. It is an edible seaweed that is harvested in the summer from Grand Manan Island, where it grows on the rocks.

The Malpeque oysters of Prince Edward Island make a rich soup called oyster bisque, while plentiful fresh lobsters often end up on PEI dinner tables—steamed, boiled, added to salads, or made into delicious lobster thermidor and accompanied by PEI's famous potatoes.

HAUTE CUISINE

Everybody knows that the French and food go together, and it is the same for French-Canadians too. Few would disagree that the two best cities in Canada for good French restaurants are Montreal and Quebec City. Many of these restaurants used to serve mainly fancy French food, or *haute cuisine*, such as *coq au vin* (chicken simmered in Burgundy wine) and *paté de foie gras* (an appetizer made of goose livers), but they now recognize that traditional French-Canadian country food has its place on their menus too.

Quebec has added *tourtière* (a meat pie), maple syrup, sugar pie (made with real maple sugar), cretons (a meat spread for sandwiches), and Oka cheese—to name just a few.

COSMOPOLITAN ONTARIO

Ontario, especially Toronto, is the most cosmopolitan region of the country. It has attracted immigrants from all over the world who have given it everything in terms of food—from solid English steak and kidney to delicate Italian capellini. British settlers preserved a love for creamed kippers and minced lamb pie even as they learned to appreciate more exotic foods. Italians, mainly from southern Italy, came after World War II and opened up shops selling blocks of Parmesan cheese, bins full of olives, and vegetables like artichokes and zucchini. Hungarians, Yugoslavs, Poles, and Rumanians added their own variations of dumplings, stews with cabbage, and sauerkraut.

A night out for *haute cuisine* in some of Quebec's more expensive French restaurants.

117

PICK YOUR OWN

Some farms and orchards encourage people to pick their own fruit. This is advertised by a roadside sign. Many people love to make a family outing out of harvesting their own fruit from a nearby farm. By picking your own, you see to it that you get just what you want. There is a certain etiquette that should be followed. Most farmers don't mind if you eat some fruit while picking, but you should not put more in your mouth than in the bucket. Children are welcome, but parents should see that their children do not disturb other pickers or run around wild. If you have never picked your own fruit, the farmer will gladly show you the best way of doing it, which varies according to the fruit.

A bishop in the Yukon, Isaac O. Stringer, discovered that when one is starving one will eat anything. Back in 1909, he and his companion became lost but survived their ordeal, thanks to their sealskin boots, which they toasted and boiled!

NORTH AND NATIVE

The North is invariably linked with frontier living and wildlife. Game food forms a large part of the local diet in both the Yukon and the Northwest Territories, where hunting, fishing, and trapping activities still occur.

Frontier food can be tough if one has to rely on moose meat, which is reputedly gamey and must be marinated for as long as one to two days before being cooked. But visitors to the north can dine well in the larger cities of Whitehorse and Yellowknife, where Alaska king crab and Yukon River salmon are specialities.

Canadian natives have special foods made from the meat of game animals (like rabbit, deer, moose, bear, buffalo, and beaver), seafood (like dried and smoked salmon, trout, cod, octopus, crabs, mussels, and clams), and wild fruit and berries. They gather varieties of wild onions, leeks, thyme, and mint, plus wood chips from cedar, maple, and hickory, and even pine cones to flavor their food. The tribes used to grow many varieties of corn and thus cooked a lot with corn flour or cornmeal. Bannock is the name for Indian bread, easily made with flour, water, and a little seasoning (see opposite).

THIRST QUENCHERS

In Canada, tea and coffee is drunk in the morning, after meals, or all day long. Children consume milk, fruit juices, and chocolate-flavored drinks. Carbonated soft drinks, or pop, as Canadians say, such as Coca-Cola, Seven-Up 'and, of course, Canada Dry, are available everywhere.

Canada produces its own wine, beer, and whisky. It has two main wine-producing regions: southwestern Ontario, especially the Niagara region, and the Okanagan in the interior of British Columbia. Several large manufacturers produce many brands of Canadian beer. There are also small local breweries, called "micro breweries," that sell their beer through special "brew-pubs." Many Canadians are also avid beer and wine makers, producing beverages ranging from excellent to dubious quality in the basements of their homes.

What better way to relax than by enjoying a glass of beer in a cafe at lunch time?

A RECIPE: BANNOCK

This is an easy way to make native Indian bread. Corn flour or cornmeal should be used, but wheat flour makes a good substitute. The ingredients are:

1 cup of plain or all-purpose flour
half teaspoon of baking powder
quarter teaspoon of salt

3 tablespoons of vegetable oil
one-third cup of water
some oil for frying

Mix the flour, baking powder, and salt together. Add the three tablespoons of oil and mix well. Add the water and knead the dough well. Heat some oil in a frying pan. When it is hot, spread the dough mixture in the pan and fry until golden brown. Serve hot. It is delicious eaten with anything. When spread with jam, it makes an excellent breakfast.

MAPLE SYRUP

Maple syrup is harvested in both Quebec and Ontario in the early springtime, when the days are warm and the nights are cold. This is when the sap rises from the roots of the tree and can be "sugared off." Mature maple trees are tapped by driving a spigot into the side of the tree. A bucket or plastic tube attached to the spigot collects the sap, which is sweet but thin. In order to make just a gallon of syrup, about 40 times the amount of sap has to be collected, placed in special containers and boiled until the syrup is sufficiently thick. "Sugaring off" is a great social event that involves everybody in the village. Children love it because they can enjoy a special treat called "sugar on snow"—chewy bits of toffee made by splashing some of the hot, thick maple syrup onto the clean snow still on the ground.

Canadians of all ages love "sugaring off."

POT LUCK

The pot-luck supper is a popular method of entertaining a large number of people. It is favored by many groups and organizations that wish to have a social evening without encountering the headaches and expense of having to feed many hungry people. Guests at a pot-luck supper are expected to bring a dish to contribute to the dining table. A good rule of thumb for knowing how much to bring is to make sure it is enough to feed your own family. Everyone then gets to taste an infinite variety and abundance of foods, making the dinner a great food adventure.

A BC MIX

Chinese, Japanese, Indian, and many other Asian immigrants form large, visible minorities in the province of British Columbia, especially in Vancouver, and have added their exotic food to Canadian cuisine. Common Asian foods like tofu, noodles, curry, and spices, such as cumin and cardamom, can now be found on supermarket shelves.

BC is also known for the variety and quality of its fish. There are five varieties of salmon—the chum, coho, pink, sockeye, and spring salmon— and huge quantities of them are caught every year and reach the market fresh, smoked, and canned. A major BC tourist attraction is the Adams River sockeye salmon run (pictured above). It occurs every year in October, when millions of adult salmon from the Pacific Ocean find their way upriver to their spawning grounds in the Adams River. There they mate, spawn, and die. Every four years, the salmon run reaches its peak. So many salmon come that they turn the water red with their color.

The market gardens and orchards produce a wealth of fruit. Loganberries, a cross between raspberries and blackberries grown on Vancouver Island, and giant Zucca melons are two special fruits seldom found anywhere outside the province.

FOOD BANKS

Most Canadians have plenty to eat, but as in practically every country in the world, even one like Canada that is so rich in resources, there are people who do not have enough money to feed themselves or their families. Canadians try to do something about these less fortunate people through food banks that are often run by charitable organizations and volunteer help. The Canadian Food Bank Association estimates that the food banks, which provide free meals and groceries to the needy, feed about 1 million people per month and distribute groceries worth $18.4 million each month.

"Screech" is the name for Newfoundland's famous dark rum and has an inspired tradition, the "screech-in," a ritual in which the visitor to the province has to down a shot of screech, kiss a codfish, then recite something in the strong accent of the Newfound-lander. The visitor is then dubbed a member of the Royal Order of Screechers and given a certificate!

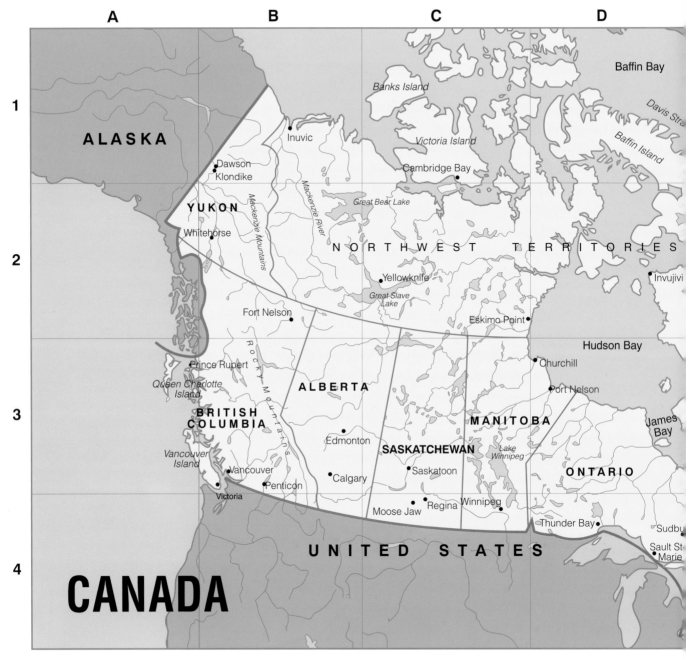

CANADA

E   F

GREENLAND

Pangnirtung

ATLANTIC
OCEAN

N E W F O U N D L A N D

UEBEC

St. John's

Gulf of
St. Lawrence

St. Lawrence River

PRINCE
EDWARD
ISLAND

Charlottetown

NEW
BRUNSWICK

NOVA SCOTIA

Quebec
City

Fredericton

Saint John

Halifax

Montreal

OTTAWA
Kingston

Toronto
tchener

Niagara Falls

N

Niagara Falls   E4
Northwest Territories   C2
Nova Scotia   F4

Ontario   D3
Ottawa   E4

Pangnirtung   E1
Penticon   B3
Port Nelson   D3
Prince Edward Island   F3
Prince Rupert   A3

Quebec City   E4
Quebec   E3
Queen Charlotte Island   A3

Regina   C4
Rocky Mountains   B3

Saint John   E4
Saskatchewan   C3

Saskatoon   C3
Sault Ste. Marie   D4
St. John's   F3
St. Lawrence River   E3
Sudbury   D4

Thunder Bay   D4
Toronto   E4

United States   C4

Vancouver   B3
Vancouver Island   A3
Victoria   B3
Victoria Island   C1

Whitehorse   B2
Winnipeg   C4

Yellowknife   C2
Yukon   B2

—— *International Boundary*

—— *State Boundary*

▲ *Mountain*

● *Capital*

● *City*

～ *River*

Lake

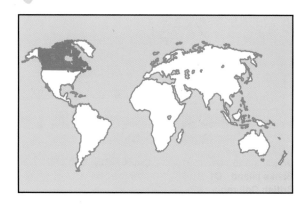

James Bay   D3

Kingston   E4
Kitchener   E4
Klondike   B1

Lake Winnipeg   C3

Mackenzie Mountains   B2
Mackenzie River   B2
Manitoba   C3
Montreal   E4
Moose Jaw   C4

New Brunswick   E3
Newfoundland   E2

QUICK NOTES

LAND AREA
3,849,652 sq miles

POPULATION
27 million

CAPITAL
Ottawa, Ontario

PROVINCES (Population in brackets)
Newfoundland (571,700), Prince Edward Island (129,900), Nova Scotia (897,900), New Brunswick (725,600), Quebec (6,811,800), Ontario (9,840,300), Manitoba (1,092,600), Saskatchewan (995,300), Alberta (2,501,400), British Columbia (3,185,900), Yukon (25,000), Northwest Territories (52,000)

NATIONAL SYMBOLS
The maple leaf and the beaver

HIGHEST POINT
Mt. Logan (19,524 ft.)

OFFICIAL LANGUAGES
English and French

MAJOR RELIGIONS
Christianity (46% Roman Catholic, 16% United Church, 10% Anglican)

CURRENCY
Canadian dollars and cents ($1 = Canadian $1.27, December 1992)

MAIN EXPORTS
Newsprint, wood pulp, timber, grain, crude petroleum, natural gas, ferrous and non-ferrous ores, motor vehicles

IMPORTANT ANNIVERSARIES
Canada Day, July 1, celebrates the Confederation of Canada in 1867
Remembrance Day, November 11

POLITICAL LEADERS
George-Etienne Cartier (1814–1873), leading French-Canadian Father of the Confederation; joint premier of United Canada (1857–62).
John A. MacDonald (1815–1892), first prime minister of Canada.
Brian Mulroney (1939–), prime minister 1984–1993.
Jacques Parizeau (1930–), leader of the Parti Québécois since 1987.
Pierre Trudeau (1919–), prime minister from 1968–79, 1980–84. Brought about the constitutional reform enabling Parliament to amend the constitution without having to appeal to the U.K. government.

GLOSSARY

boggataway An Indian game, eventually developed by Canadian settlers into lacrosse, used to develop group discipline and personal ingenuity.

canuck Slang for Canadian.

Crown land Land belonging to the public.

haute cuisine Fine food prepared in an elaborate manner.

Inuit The native people, also called eskimos, who inhabit the northern, Arctic regions of Canada and Greenland.

kayak A light boat made of sealskin or man-made material.

muskeg Bog or marshy land.

New France The name given to the French-controlled area of North America (until 1763), encompassing a part of the United States and Canada.

potlatch Indian gift of money or goods.

powwow Indian ritual healing ceremony.

proselytize Convert from one belief to another.

reservations A tract of land set aside for the use of Indian people.

riding An electoral district.

tithe A tax (usually 10%), to support clergy and church.

BIBLIOGRAPHY

Canada Year Book, Statistics Canada, Ottawa, 1992.

Hacker, Carlotta: *The Book of Canadians: An Illustrated Guide to Who Did What,* Hurtig Publishers, Edmonton, 1983.

Lunn, Janet, and Moore, Christopher: *The Story of Canada,* Lester Publishing and Key Porter Books, Toronto, 1992.

Malcolm, Andrew: *The Canadians,* Fitzhenry and Whiteside, Markham, Ontario, 1985.

Richardson, Bill: *Canada Customs: Droll Recollections, Musings and Quibbles,* Brighouse Press, Vancouver, 1988.

Watson, Jessie and Wreford: *The Canadians: How they live and work,* Griffin Press Ltd., Toronto, 1977.

Woodcock, George: *The Canadians,* Fitzhenry and Whiteside, Don Mills, Ontario, 1979.

INDEX

INDEX

INDEX

PICTURE CREDITS
APA: 10, 12, 13, 20, 51, 54, 58, 78, 94
British High Commission, Singapore: 36
Canada Asean Centre/Alberta Tourism: 1, 5, 17
Canada Asian Centre/Isolde Ohlbaum: 92
Canada Asean Centre/ISTC: 4, 6, 8, 15, 44, 74, 84, 103,
    110, 111, 116, 120
Canada Asean Centre/Province of British Columbia: 102
Hulton-Deutsch: 25, 30, 37, 40, 97
Hutchison Library: 26, 68, 107, 121
Image Bank: 9, 11, 14, 18, 27, 31, 34, 38, 43, 45, 46, 47,
    48, 49, 55, 56, 76, 80, 90, 98, 100, 101, 106, 108, 109,
    112, 114, 117, 118
Life File Photo Library: 3, 16, 50, 64
David Simson: 32, 33, 42, 52, 57, 59, 60, 61, 62, 66, 67,
    69, 70, 72, 73, 75, 82, 83, 85, 86, 87, 88, 91, 95, 96,
    104, 105, 115, 119